April 7 2012

To Dave and Kathy — Thanks a lot — My best regard —

Charlotte

STERLING

BY
Charlotte Crawford

To Order
1-888-232-4444

Order this book online at www.trafford.com
or email orders@trafford.com

Most Trafford titles are also available at major online book retailers.

© Copyright 2011 Charlotte Crawford.
All rights reserved. No part of this publication may be reproduced, stored
in a retrieval system, or transmitted, in any form or by any means, electronic,
mechanical, photocopying, recording, or otherwise, without
the written prior permission of the author.

Printed in the United States of America.

ISBN: 978-1-4269-6506-7 (sc)
ISBN: 978-1-4269-6507-4 (e)

Library of Congress Control Number: 2011905735

Trafford rev. 08/18/2011

 www.trafford.com

North America & international
toll-free: 1 888 232 4444 (USA & Canada)
phone: 250 383 6864 ♦ fax: 812 355 4082

TABLE OF CONTENTS

This Is Sterling	1
Save My Seat	32
The Coyote Kids	43
Walk With The Girl	62
The Great Walk	68
Miz Lerner	87
The Twins	96
The Fire	105
Burris Sickle	110
Sister Phoebe's And Uncle Jake's Home	115
The Murder	118
The Funeral	121
The Trial	124
The Last Page	130
About the Author	133

Dedicated
to
my
childhood
friends
and
Roy Rogers
and
Trigger

Thank you

Let it be known: all Scots-Irish people who migrated to the Southern states are Crackers, rich and poor alike and the only acceptable and accurate definition of Cracker is: people of excellence who tell great stories and have a lot to boast about - especially their food.

The saddest commentary about the word is all the negative connotations it has been given over the generations here in the United States. The latest blow was the death knell dealt to it during the civil rights struggles in the 1960's. People and the press needed a nick-name for the Southern racial bigots. The word "Cracker" was the handiest, even won out over "red-neck". These people should check their history, dictionaries and talk to people from Great Britain. They will find out they are sorely mistaken. They took a whack out of our identity.

This author has also grown weary of the Frederick Remingtoils drawings of Crackers or cow hunters with the droopy-head-hanging-down horse, the droopy-head-hanging-down cow poke, with the

THIS IS STERLING

Once in a great, great while the right people come together at the right time, at the right place to form a community that can only be described as sheer magic. That place was the town of Sterling.

We were ten years old. It was 1947- that wholesome, most pleasant, adventurous, refreshing period of time between World War II and television that will never be improved upon.

We were riding high and mighty on a great wave of heroes. We won the war and everyone was brave. The soldiers fought the war and we helped. We had victory gardens, endured rationing and air raid drills, sent care packages, had scrap metal drives and bought war bonds.

Sterling was not the largest town in the county but we won the award for collecting the most scrap metal. We even took down the heavy iron stop signs and replaced them with wooden ones. That is what put us in first place.

We brought dimes to school and bought stamps we stuck into little booklets. Some of the stamps had pictures of army tanks or airplanes. When the booklet was full we traded it in for a war bond that was worth $18.75. In ten years it would be worth $25.00. I still had seven years to go on mine.

We believed in our town, ourselves and each other. We believed everything was good or on its way to getting good because that was the way everyone wanted it. We believed if you showed someone the right thing to do and the wrong thing to do they would choose the right thing to do. We believed everyone wanted to be good - that everyone wanted to be a hero. We believed it was the good peoples' job to make the bad people behave. Like the good cowboys in the movies who made the bad cowboys straighten up or go to jail. At school our teachers were sincere and the movies gave us our most noble heroes of all: Roy Rogers and Trigger.

If this period of time was created for children then the place that was created for children was the town of Sterling. It could not have been better if it had been staged by a big movie producer - like Cecile B. DeMille. The population was about eight thousand. Just right. Even the physical layout of the town was ideal.

The very heart of downtown was about five blocks by seven blocks. Contained in that thirty-five blocks was all the material things and everything else we needed for our warmth, security, adventure and wonderment - activities - community and just plain fun and happiness.

There were three drug stores with full fountains, two large five and dime stores we browsed through everyday, four grocery stores, a fish market, four restaurants, five stores selling clothes for men, women and children, a large hardware store that sold everything including bridles and saddle for our horses. Beauty parlors, barbershops, an ice cream shop, an auto supply store, a bicycle shop, a gift shop that even sold china and silver, an office supply store, a news stand where we bought our precious comic books.

They were ten cents each. There was a gun shop that we were so fascinated with we even enjoyed just walking past it. A big bank where everyone kept all their money. I had eleven dollars in there. There was a shoe shop that put new bottoms on my old tops, a taxi stand, a camera shop, appliance stores, furniture stores and a feed store for the cows and horses.

There were baseball gloves, b-b guns, bicycles, model airplanes, cap pistols, roller skates, kites and fun things galore just waiting for us to scrape up the money so we could adopt them and take them home with us.

There was a music store that sold records and sheet music owned by a man that knew everything about music. He could come up with any record we asked for. He was a pro - played saxophone at dances at the pavilion at the big lake north of town. One of the three jewelry stores sold musical instruments. There were lots and lots of merchants, doctors, lawyers and maybe even an Indian Chief. People were dazzled by the number of churches. More than we could count. Dozens. And there were just as many gas stations, maybe even more.

There was a civic center with a big pool where we spent happy, splashy summer days. It cost ten cents to swim. Most important of all there was a movie theatre where we spent a thousand afternoons riding the magic carpet of blessed cinema. When our heroes rode their majestic horses across the screen we rode up there right along side them. It cost nine cents to go to the movies.

There was a three story hotel that looked like it was from a hundred years ago. It had its own row of nine shops along one side with a radio repair shop that was headquarters for model airplanes that could fly all by themselves.

The lobby of the hotel was a huge cavern with big square columns. Everything was brown or tan. There was not much light. It was curious. On the further end there was a staircase that rose up then split into two cases. One went to the left, the other to the right. This was a movie set if there ever was one. Every inch of that lobby spelled i-n-t-r-i-g-u-e. There were oriental rugs we had never seen before. The man behind the counter was tall, very thin and pale as a ghost. He wore a black suit and a black bow tie. We swear we saw the actor, Sidney Greenstreet, sitting in one of the high back chairs peeking at us over his newspaper.

The grapevine had told us that the first bubble gum for sale since the war was at the hotel. This is strange in itself. The only thing that was for sale in that lobby was a box of bubble gum sitting on that bare counter. My friend Loren, the boy genius who was born knowing everything, said that place was indeed strange. The bubble gum was one cent each. I had three cents. Loren had four cents. We skeedaddled out of there with our seven pieces and chewed and blew that day until our jaws were so sore we could not sleep that night. The pale man never said a word to us. We were not sure if he was real or what. But from that day on we would slip into the hotel and explore around each floor and hallway and banquet room. We would walk around thinking "Okay. Go ahead and scare us!" We loved the anticipation. We were so brave.

Above the third floor was a look-out tower. We could see the whole town from up there. We figured this was about as high up as anyone could be and still be in a building.

Our friend we called Else (because he was always doing something odd, something other than what the rest of us were doing, something else) climbed up on the roof of the tower and flew a kite from there. We looked up one day and there he was, flying his kite wwwaaaaayyy up high. Adventure had no limit and Else was not afraid of anything.

Across the street from the hotel there was the library. The library building seemed ancient and as fascinating as the books in it. There was a musty old basement where the original librarians repaired and rebound books. There was even an old book binding machine down there. We were not supposed to know about the basement but we snuck down there one day. It was scary. Like "Intersanctum", the radio show. Upstairs there were wooden columns and beams across the ceiling, wooden floors with a strip of carpet in front of the counter. There was a fireplace over in the corner away from the books. Cozy.

The library was the quietest place we ever went. We were not allowed to talk. We had to whisper. The librarian sat up high at the counter. She seemed to go with the building. She loomed over us. She whispered so low we could barely hear her. We had to read her lips. We called her "Whisperer's mother". But, she had great reading programs for kids. For each book we read she would stick a gold star onto a cardboard cut-out of a cowboy. One on each spur, one on each gun, one on his hat, one on his chest. We really liked gold stars and would do most anything to earn them.

A little way down the street was the newspaper office and print shop. Big double doors opened onto the sidewalk. We would stand out there and watch the papers roll off the press. The thing was so big and shook so hard we could feel the vibrations of the sidewalk under our feet. We felt like we were a part of the publication.

Some businesses were not just businesses. They were lifetime apexes. Like the bakery. Anyone who had ever lived in Sterling knew about the rectangular shaped donut type, white iced "Long Johns". Those who moved away would always come to Sterling if they were anywhere nearby to get some "Long Johns". When kids played hooky from school they would always high tail it to the bakery to get some of these tasty morsels. They cost five cents each. The bakery was only two blocks from elementary school. Sometimes we would give our nickels to the janitor we called "Pop". He would go get them and bring them to us. Long Johns is the reason they invented the word "delicious".

Boys who had paper routes would ride their bikes to the bakery before daylight. The lady who owned the shop, who we called "Long John's mother", would give them a sack of glazed donuts still warm from the fryer. By the time they got to school they were so wound up on sugar they could not sit down. When people went for a walk late in the evening they would always walk near the bakery. This is when they baked the bread. The aroma was worth the walk.

Another favorite was the Coca Cola bottling plant. We would stand on orange crates outside the windows and marvel at the bottles being filled and flying by on the conveyor belt. It was hypnotic. If the belt stopped while we're watching we would fall over in the opposite direction the bottles had been moving. Loren tried to explain this to us but we still did not quite understand.

There were houses sprinkled all through downtown. Many of the buildings had offices or apartments upstairs. A very cozy way to live. A lot of people in Sterling did not have cars. They did not need them. Everything was in walking distance. The adults loved living in Sterling as much as the children did.

There was usually a lot of people downtown during the week. On Saturdays the town was packed jam full. Some people only came to town on Saturday. This is what they looked forward to. Going to town on Saturday to see everyone.

A big important day. It was called "country come to town". Some people would go to town in the afternoon and park their car in a good spot then walk home, eat an early supper then walk back to the car and sit there all evening. The cars were parked nose first against the curb. We loved to "watch the people go by". Many would stop and talk and visit through the window. There were so many shoppers and the stores were so busy most of them stayed open until ten or eleven o'clock. Some stores did half of their business on Saturdays.

We always had something to look forward to. That is what made Sterling such a wonderful place to live. We always had something to look forward to and children never had to wonder: "Where were the people who were supposed to take care of us?" We were never out of the sight of caring eyes. When we would walk to town there would be people sitting on their front porches. We knew them and they knew us. We were protected by the whole town.

We were not just members of a community. We belonged to a clan. Most of the people who originally settled here were Scots - Irish immigrants. Although, a few were very British.

The Scots - Irish were clannish. They migrated here because their ways had become threatened in Scotland and Ireland. They came to America for freedom and independence so they could hang onto their ways and be happy. This is what my father said. And he was a lawyer so he oughta know. Our Scots - Irish Southerners were Scot - Irish Southerners long before they got here. They had been preparing to be clanish Southerners for centuries.

The phosphate mines drew droves of immigrants to the area of Sterling. There were several phosphate villages a few miles from town. These villages were the homiest places anyone could live and were a fine example of clanism. The people who lived there were very close and looked out for each other. The villages were a very safe place to raise children.

The largest village to the south had several hundred people living there, a large commissary, a drug store, movie theatre, a clinic, a high school with a football team, a spring fed swimming pool. All the villages had a post office and a commissary and even the smallest had some kind of recreational facilities - maybe a nine hole golf course or a lake for swimming and picnics - all free to the employees. People loved living in the villages. They felt very much at home there because they were at home and they knew it. Kids who lived in town loved to go to visit their friends in the villages. It was like a different world out there and we could feel the specialness. Most of the kids attended school in Sterling. When families came into town on Saturday they usually came into Sterling rather than the towns several miles in other directions. The villagers felt at home in Sterling. They were all sister cities.

Sterling was smack kadab in the middle of the middle of the State of Florida. It was a combination of a tropical rain forest and Texas cattle country. People migrated down here to work in the citrus groves, turpentine forests, phosphate mines and the cattle ranches. These were all really big businesses. A lot of them worked their way down here building the railroad. That is how a lot of the colored people got here.

Sterling was situated in the middle of a thick oak hammock. Long ago Indians and then soldiers camped here when there was nothing here except trees. East of town a big long river ran from north to south. The Indians and then soldiers used the river for water, fishing, their boats and for their general comfort. We were still using the river for the same reasons.

The Indians were the first to come here. Soldiers liked the trees so much they came back and brought their families with them. They told the Indians they had to leave - they had lived under the trees long enough and now it was the soldiers and other peoples' turn. Or something like that. They fought but the soldiers won. This was way back. Even before the civil war. After the war everyone who came here wanted to live under the trees. There were still a few Indians living way, way out in the woods and in the swamp. Once in a while we would see them.

Sterling was the name of a very wealthy, well educated general in the Confederate Calvary. He and the Calvary brought herds of horses with them. The town was still full of horses. Someone once said there were almost as many horses in Sterling as there were people. Homes had large yards. Most of the old timey houses that were first built were still here. About every tenth house had an extra acre or two with a horse lot and a small barn. There were horses and cows two blocks from Main Street. A dairy next to the high school about ten blocks south of downtown with a huge pasture, lots of cows and horses. The owners would rent us a pony for 25 cents. There were little farms sprinkled all over town. We rode horses just about everywhere. We loved our cowboy and horse heroes in the movies and we rode our fantasies right into reality.

More and more people migrated here, liked what they saw and stayed longer and longer forming the little town known as "the city in the woods". People who lived in Sterling lived in town and in the country at the same time.

Irish immigrants came searching for a living. British nobility came here to invest in land, lots of land. Cubans came here to get away from Cuba and to grow tobacco and roll cigars. The farmers grew vegetables in the rich earth fertilized by the phosphate not far below the surface. There were miles and miles of citrus groves.

Many of the people who originally settled in Sterling were very wealthy, well educated people who sent their children to liberal arts colleges. Then their children would come back to Sterling to keep the culture going. There was a tremendous amount of activity in music, art, theatre and everything else that was interesting.

Our generation saw a high school chorus that could sing "The Messiah" without the books.

These were children age 14 to 18. We did not know choruses at other schools could not sing "The Messiah" at all with or without books. The chorus teacher worked very hard. The kids in the chorus worked even harder. They always won superior ratings at chorus contests.

There was a Music Club, Art Guild, a theatre group and service clubs of every description. Every moment of every day was vital. Everything was within our capabilities. We had it all. We did it all. Sterling was filled with drama, objectivity, creativity, production and passion. And there was music everywhere.

The first big building in Sterling was a bank building. The second big building was an opera house. Throughout the decades the people of Sterling always cherished anything that took place on a stage and sounded anything like music.

Most of all, it seemed like everyone put children first. There were summer programs at the civic center, the library, churches and Scouts and a Halloween Parade and carnival. They were all for us. Even the fountains at the drug stores catered to our taste. Cherry Coke.

On the day Sterling became a city it all began with a parade with food and festivities at the end of the parade. That tradition continued. Parades and food and food and parades.

The most important thing in Sterling was food. No one questioned thanking God at the dinner table. Food made everything possible. Where there was activity there was food. Where there was food there was activity

When Haley's comet passed by in 1910 people in town got out of bed in the middle of the night, put on hats and coats, went out in the chilly night to the original high school that was more like a small private college. The professor who taught astronomy had a telescope. There were tables of coffee and hot chocolate and muffins. They stood in line and took turns watching the spectacular sight pass by. They did this two nights in a row. No one seemed to think this was difficult. Just another good thing to do. Together.

The pulse of the town was the movie theatre and we kept our finger on that pulse. It was on Main Street right in the center of town and was by far the most attended building in Sterling.

It was built in the 1920's when movies did not have sound. The town's official piano playing lady got her start there by playing along with the good old silent movies. The piano lady played everywhere there was a piano. Church, civic clubs, musicals, weddings, operettas, recitals. When there was a program outdoors they would put her piano on the back of a flatbed truck and there she would be. If you heard a piano it was her. And, boy! She sure could play the thing. It sounded like two or three pianos all going at once. She played so much she was muscular, strong. She patted her foot so hard keeping time we could hear the whap and scrape of her shoe above her very loud piano. More amazement for us.

There were three sets of movies each week. Regular movies Sunday, Monday and Tuesday. Another set on Wednesday and Thursday. Friday and Saturday was the cowboy, cartoons, serials, double features for kids.

Some of us saw every movie. During the week we would leave school and beat a path to the three o'clock show. It was only four blocks away. We ran like a herd of wild horses. We would sit through some movies a half dozen times if we were particularly smitten by them. On a couple of school nights our parents came in and got us after ten p.m. A swashbuckler starring John Barrymore, Jr. This did not happen very often but the fact it happened at all tells us the quality of the movies and how much they meant to us. The movies fit the town and the people.

We kids lined up around the block on Saturdays waiting for the box office to open at 12:45 p.m. We loved the movies and we also had a gigantic passion for being stuffed in that theatre shoulder to shoulder with each other.

The entrance was narrow, then opened up into the lobby, then opened up into the main room of about four hundred seats. We were a huge litter of puppies gathered in the womb of this mother of fantasy. When we spewed out after the show it was like a birth renewal. No matter how good we felt when we went in we always felt even better when we came out.

The drugstore on the corner of Main Street and Central Avenue was a magnet for all ages, especially for young people and teenagers. Of course, there were a lot of older people who went there every day. The owner - pharmacist was a master story teller. When he had time he would come out among the tables and tell the most interesting stories we had ever heard. It did not matter if they were true or not. We believed him. That is what made them true. We would sit at the tables with our cokes, sundaes and sandwiches and enjoy the floor show. It was great theatre.

There was also plenty of room to stand around on the sidewalk outside. When soldiers came home on leave they went to several places but they always went to the drug store on the corner. They knew that was where they would see familiar faces. After World War II ended and all the soldiers came home the corner was filled to the brim. Some stood around in their uniforms because they wanted to and others because they had grown so much during the war they no longer had civilian clothes that fit. Some of their shirts had thread outlines. Corporal stripes and sergeant stripes. Then most of them would go to the movie theatre later that afternoon.

The movie theatre was where almost everyone in town went regularly and where they would rally when something happened that had to be dealt with. Like a war or something. There was a school bus accident coming back from a football game. It was the band bus. One student died. Several were seriously injured. All were bent and bruised. This was on a Friday night, very late. By the next afternoon most of the bent and bruised we were at the theatre for the Saturday matinee - walking up and down the aisles saying "hey" to their friends.

Each person had their favorite spots to go downtown and we all went from place to place like honeybees gathering nourishment from sweet flowers.

The first stage built in Sterling was the opera house. This was way back a long time ago. Professional opera companies came there. Don't know what happened to this theatre. It may have burned down like a lot of those old wood buildings. Seems like they were built to eventually burn down. Don't think any of them were torn down. Sometime in maybe the 1920's they built a big huge theatre building out of concrete near the elementary school. It was gigantic and very fancy. Maybe about eight-hundred seats with a big balcony. As a theatre it was as good as they came. Sterling was probably the only little bitsy town that had such a place. Real traveling shows came there. Vaudeville. It eventually became known as the city auditorium.

Movies took place at the movie theatre. Everything else took place at the city auditorium. Graduation ceremonies, band concerts, music and dance recitals, talent shows, all the school plays, Rotary Club minstrals. Any gathering that required a stage. We saw the incredible operettas there. The music teacher who directed "The Messiah" also directed the operettas. It was electrifying to hear those high school students sing like professional adults. We did not know other schools did not have a Messiah chorus or an operetta troupe. All we knew is that when we came out of that theatre after we had been taken over to watch dress rehearsals of the operettas, we were flying about three feet off the ground - especially my best friend "Melody", the musical genius. She would be singing all the songs - on key - all the right words - as she always did when we saw a movie that was a musical. Our teacher, Miz Lerner, said she was a prodigy. Her sister we called "Two Pound" could do the same thing and she was as smart as Loren. We all called her "Two Pound" because she only weighed two pounds when she was born and she did not look to be much bigger now. Melody was a little older than the rest of us. Two Pound was a little younger.

We did not know how unique we were and how unique our surroundings were. People in Sterling enjoyed themselves and each other to the 'nth degree. We entertained each other and we were each others' audience.

By far the most majestic building in Sterling was the court house. We identified with it and it was the landmark for everyone who had ever lived in Sterling. It impressed people who had only been there once, always to remember the little town with the big court house. We did not believe buildings ever got much bigger. It was about four stories counting the huge dome that held the clock with faces on all four sides. A loud gong rang for each hour of what ever time it was. It told us when to go and what to do. Eight gongs meant it was about time for school or work. Twelve gongs meant it was time for the noon meal. Three gongs meant the weekday movie was about to begin. The court house guided us by sight and sound.

When we went out of town it was always a warming sight to see the dome coming up as we were still a few miles out on the highway. When we saw the dome on the court house we knew we were almost home. It was our touch stone. And it was good.

At Christmas they would cover the dome in big holiday lights. We could then see the dome even farther away. The lighted dome made Christmas be Christmas for miles and miles. It gave people who did not have much Christmas some of the celebration everyone else had.

The silver eagle in flight on the lighting rod on top of the dome looked just like the eagle that was the logo of Republic Pictures. They made the Roy Rogers and Trigger movies. The roof on the dome was silver and shinny just like the sterling silver trim on Trigger's saddle and bridle and on Roy's gun belt and holsters. They all seemed to be connected. And, the clock told us when it was time to go to the movies.

The big old building was a source of fascination for kids and for adults, too. There was a basement with secret narrow stairways - sounds that went bump in the dark - attic rooms on the third floor with their own sinister stair cases. And, everyone in town believed there was a ghost up there. If there wasn't there should have been. Ghosts were missing a dang good chance if they did not live on the third floor or in the dome of the court house.

Our friend, Slip, loved the courthouse. He was always slipping around peeking around corners or from behind a bush. He thought he was Dick Tracy, Sherlock Holmes, Charlie Chan, Boston

Blackie and Sam Spade all rolled up into one. He did not say much. Just slipped around.

Very few, if any, would dare crawl up the ladder stairs to the dome where the big clock machinery was. We went up high enough one day just to see some of the weights, pullies and gears. Mostly just workmen went up there. During the war air raid wardens would go outside and stand on the balcony that surrounded the dome to look for enemy airplanes. The people who went up these days was mostly the custodian, Mosey, and his helper, Quick Step. They went up there to wind a big spring that ran the clock and maybe to oil something.

The whole building inside and out, especially the court rooms, looked like something we might see in the movies. The windows were usually kept open during the day except in real cold weather. We could stand on the sidewalk or the porch and talk to the people working in the offices. A lot of kids had parents who worked there. We would play in the yard of the court house while the parents watched us. Sometimes they would toss us a quarter to finance our next adventure.

The second floor had a huge round hole in the very center of it. We could stand on the first floor and look up to the bottom of the third floor. And that is exactly what we would do - stand there and look up. And, we wondered why the heck they would build something like that. But we were glad they did.

It stands to reason that the court house was where the greatest adventure of our young lives would soon take place.

The court house was the largest building where legal stuff took place. Across the street from the court on the corner under one of the big oak trees was the smallest official building in the world. It was concrete, about six feet by eight feet inside. It was just barely big enough for one desk and one chair. There was a candle stick telephone on the desk. That was the only things in there. It had two screen doors and two windows. This was the police station. Previously, the police station was a wooden box nailed to the tree with the telephone inside it. The telephone seldom rang. When it did ring someone nearby may or may not have answered it. They might take a message and give it to a policeman the next time they saw him. There were three policemen in the 1930's. They took turns being chief. The chief got to wear the uniform with the real brass buttons.

After they built the little building there might be a policeman sitting in there once in a while. On Saturdays the phone rang more and got answered more because men would bring chairs from the buildings and sit on the sidewalk next to the little building under the big oak tree. If the phone rang one of the men would answer it. Maybe. There were plans to move the police station to a red brick house about two blocks from Main Street. But, there did not seem to be much hurry. There really was not much crime in Sterling anymore. There used to be long, long, ago. But not now.

Way back before the nineteen hundreds there was a group of men who were like a posse. They were more like vigilantes. They called themselves "regulators". They made everyone want to behave and behave they did. And they rode horses, too.

One time two bad cowboys came riding into town. They were no where near sober and they were running around, picking fights, shooting their guns and just being plain mean. The marshal came to arrest them and they shot him dead. The bad cowboys were taken and locked up in the jail that was just a room at the fire station. They were not there long before the regulators came and got them and hung them from one of the big oak trees.

Another time a very nice lady was out fishing at the creek when some man she did not even know assaulted her and beat her to death. The man's neighbors knew he had done it and brought him into town and turned him over to the deputies. The man was hanged and burned at stake. Just like Ingrid Bergman in the movie "Joan of Arc". Before they did all this most of the children in Sterling were taken a few miles south to a beautiful place called "The Springs" where there was an icy cold natural pond surrounded by big oak trees. There was a pavilion and tables under the trees. They had a picnic then came back to town late that evening. Since then there really had not been much crime in Sterling. People behaved and were very pleasant. From then on people in Sterling also felt very secure. Hardly anyone locked their doors. Sometimes they would go to bed at night and not only would they not close the wooden doors they did not even latch the screen doors.

The regulators did a good job.

There is no way to tell about Sterling without telling about the colored people. That is what we called everyone back then that were not white. Colored. And how important they were to the beginning of Sterling and its keeping on being what it was. Long ago when it came time to sign the papers to make Sterling a real city they extended the city limits line out a good ways to include one of the best farms out there. It was owned by a colored man who was one of the first people to settle there. He got there before most of the white people. They needed his vote to have enough to make Sterling a city. The church he and some of the other colored people started also started a school for the colored children. They settled a neighborhood with lots of houses and a few stores. We called this little town "Cross the Creek" because it was north of town just across the creek. The colored people did a lot for themselves with little or no help from the white people. In some ways they did more for themselves than the white people did for themselves. They had a tougher time, but they made it.

And white people here could not have possibly gotten along without the help they got from the colored people. They are the ones who kept the axles greased that made the town keep on going. The colored people were always there every step of the way.

Not all the families had colored people who worked for them but many did. They took care of houses inside and out, took care of children, were porters at the movie theatre, the custodians at the court house and post office, delivered ice and groceries, picked up the trash and garbage, picked the fruit, repaired the railroad and did a mountain of work at the phosphate mines.

Take a good look at the judge at the court house sitting on the bench with his crisp white shirt under his robe. That shirt was washed and ironed by a colored lady. He left a nice clean house and would go home to a delicious meal all done by a colored lady. The lawn at his house was as neat as a pin because a colored man made it that way. A lot would not have gotten done if colored people had not have done it. Seems like they really cared about us and took us to raise because they thought we could not take care of ourselves. Children and nannies became very close. Our life was a lot better with colored people than it would have been without them.

And it always seemed colored people knew a lot more than what they told us. We learned a lot from them but it seemed there was a lot more they could have taught us. It seemed they made it a point not to let us know how smart they really were. My grandmother said they did not want us to know everything they knew. This was their way of keeping one step ahead of us. And she oughta know. She was the wisest person who ever lived. My grandfather said colored people stayed mum most of the time because they wanted to make sure they did not get misquoted. And he oughta know. He was the superintendent at the mines. It is not surprising that it was a young colored man who helped us get through the most horrible thing that ever happened in Sterling.

For each very wealthy person in Sterling there was a very poor person and everyone else in between. They all seemed to blend. We could not tell the rich ones from the poor ones. They all acted pretty much the same. This goes back to the clannishness of the Scots-Irish people. It is difficult to explain but very easy to accept That was the way it was and that was the way we liked it. My father said we were Crackers. I did not know exactly what that meant but I figured it must be something mighty good.

The place, the time and the people all went together. It was a perfect match. All this is why we believed in each other, ourselves, our heroes and the town. We believed in anything that had anything to do with Sterling. It was where playmates grew up to be soul mates. We loved the time, the place and the people. The luckiest people in the world are the children who grew up in Sterling during the 1940's and 1950's.

Yes, everything in Sterling was just perfect. Except for one thing. The undertaker was killing people.

SAVE MY SEAT

Save my seat. This is what we always told the kid sitting next to us at the movies when we would leave our perch for a while and want to make sure we had a place to sit when we came back. Our friend would save our seat and who ever might have thought of sitting there would be told, This seat is saved.

On Saturday afternoons there were always more kids in the theatre than the hundreds of seats. We could not all sit down at the same time. But that was okay because we did not want to all sit down at the same time. There were always dozens up and down the aisles, out in the lobby, at the snack bar, in and out of the restrooms, a line at the water fountain. They did not just walk up and down the slanted aisles. They would ride their imaginary horses. Sometimes trot, then gallop, then run. We could get up some real speed running down the slope. There were four aisles. Thank goodness. They still got crowded sometimes.

It looked like no one was really paying attention to the movie but they were. When one of our heroes came galloping in to save the day everyone would freeze in their tracks, sit up straight in their seats and let out a yell, Yeaaah! and clapping so loud we could be heard out the front doors and a block or two down the street. Our strongest beliefs were reinforced by our heroes. No one has ever been more secure or had a stronger sense of power than these kids at the Saturday afternoon cowboy movies. Because: This was wholesome power.

We had a passion for all our cowboy heroes: Gene Autry and Champion; Red Ryder and Thunder; Little Beaver and Papose. Loren had a list of all the cowboys and their horses.

By far and above the lot was Roy Rogers and Trigger. They fit. The horse, the man, the saddle. They melted into one. It was obvious the horse and the man were soul mates. Trigger would run so fast the wind he created lifted the long hair of his mane and tail so high they took on a life of their own. Roy Rogers had as much or more influence on us as our parents, school or church. We would have done anything he told us to do.

(One kid told us Roy Rogers and Dale Evans were his parents. How could anyone blame him for wishing this so hard it seemed to be true. As time went by we learned a lot of kids across the country told people Roy Rogers and Dale Evans were their parents.)

The music in the Roy Rogers movies was a very special, extra added bonus for us. We were already musical so Roy Rogers and Dale Evans' singing really came home to us. Roy was the first person we ever heard yodel in a movie. Everything he did seemed unique. And, there is no more a comforting sound than his group, The Sons of the Pioneers singing, Tumbleweed. We could sing it pretty good too. Although we never did learn how to yodel. Roy Rogers made us into something better than we would have been without him. He did not just tell us how to live. He showed us right up there on that screen in our tiny town.

Rule number one in the Roy Rogers cowboy club was: Never take advantage of anyone, not even your enemy. In almost every Roy Rogers movie there was a scene where the bad cowboy was about to get away. As the bad cowboy rode off

Roy would pull his gun from his holster and aim it at the bad cowboy's back...then think twice... raise the barrel of the gun...put the gun back into his holster...jump on Trigger and away they would go in hot pursuit. Trigger could out run all the bad horses. Roy would jump from Trigger onto the bad horse and bad cowboy...knock him to the ground...fist fight and rolling around and down a hill...Roy would capture the bad cowboy by hand...not by shooting him in the back or by shooting him at all.

We were only ten years old but we knew this was noble and we knew this was the way we wanted to be. For someone to always make an effort to do the right thing then stick to their honor no matter what was known as The Code of the West. This is the way we would live. We would accept no less. We loved cowboys and horses so much we even loved saddles and bridles and saddle blankets. The big hardware store was next to the movie theatre. When we came out of the theatre we would run to the hardware store and hop on the saddles they had sitting on racks. We were a regular little posse perched on these saddles hooping and hollering and bouncing up and down in full gallop. The owners of the store never said anything to us about our raiding the tack department. They knew sooner or later we would be buying some of this riding gear for our own horses. One girl loved horses so much she even loved horse feed. She stopped by the feed store and got a handful of oats. The owner gave them to her. She lived in an upstairs apartment but there was plenty of dirt out in the yard. She planted the oats in a safe little row. We marveled at the sprigs when they sprouted up. She said, This is what horses eat. We ooohed and aaahed.

She was only ten years old but said she would marry Roy Rogers and Trigger right this minute. She was in love with every boy in town who had a horse. Did not pay much attention to boys who did not have their own horses. Time and time again she said when she grew up and got married she would marry a cowboy who had horses.

Everything was cowboys. Everything was horses. The bicycle rack in front of the gun shop was the hitching post. After the movie kids would mount up by putting their left foot on the low pedal and swinging their right leg over the seat. Just like mounting a horse. Then they would ride off into the sunset. A day well spent.

Loren and I would walk the few blocks to where we were neighbors. He had Saturday afternoons all figured out. He usually had a quarter. The movie was nine cents. He could get a small popcorn for five cents, and candy bar and coke for five cents each. (A coke in a cup from a machine. Better than nothing.) Then we would stop by the newsstand where he would get a jaw breaker for a penny for a total of twenty-five cents.

After a hard day's work at the movies and the salty, thirsty popcorn I was ready to hit the bar. At the soda fountain at the drugstore. For five cents I could get a taste and a quench of heaven in a cherry coke. When that cold, delicious, foamy, sweet tingle came through the straw and hit the back of my throat in Sterling after a few hours with my friends cheering Roy Rogers and Trigger I was as happy and as secure and as fulfilled as a kid could possibly be. This was perfection to the nth degree. This was heaven on earth and then some. Life in Sterling was total. It was whole. It was complete.

Days we did not go to the movies we spent re-enacting the movies we had seen. We weren't limited to Roy Rogers or cowboy movies. We did them all: cops and robbers, Flash Gordan,

Tarzan, pirates. We had make-shift costumes and we made the props we needed.

There was a tremendous amount of constant action. We ran around chasing and lassoing each other. Great fencing matches. We would shoot each other with our cap pistols, fall and roll down a hill. If we could find a hill. Our fake fist fights looked as real as the fake fist fights in the movies. We made verbal sound affects of fist fights, gun shots, ricochet bullets, horses hooves and whinnies. We had stick horses and buck board wagons made of saw horses, planks and orange crates. Sometimes we did this on real ponies. Dogs would join in as if they knew what was going on. They played their roles.

Tarzan was one of our most interesting scenes. We had plenty of ropes to swing on and any kid who was worth his salt could do the Tarzan yell. A really low, large, long limb served as a horse, space ship or an elephant we rode on safari. We did not mind taking turns being the much loved chimpanzee, Cheetah. Adults sitting on their front porches would watch us for as long as we did our play acting. They were watching dang good theatre. Darkness was just about the only thing that made us stop. Our parents had to force us to come inside. Sometimes we would play outside after dark as long as we did not go too far off. Darkness put an even more magic veil on everything.

We included comic book characters. Batman was a favorite. There was something about his cape, utility belt and bat mobile that was almost too fascinating. I made a cape and a utility belt. The only thing I could find to put in it was a magnifying glass, a box of matches and fingernail clippers with a tiny knife.

We even had a big flashlight with a cut-out of a bat on the lens. We would shine it on the side of buildings. Just like Batman.

When we played hide and seek after dark I would hide under my black cape beneath the hedge bushes. No one could ever find me. Then I would jump out and scare the beejeebers out of my friends. They loved it. They thought I was the greatest playmate there ever was.

All this lore was a gift to us to cherish. This period of time when children vigorously participated in everything and we designed our lives as we went along. We wrote our own scripts.

One type of movie we did not get involved in was the religion movies. We enjoyed Sunday school with the Baptists. Church services were okay. Especially the singing part. The preaching part was too long and we could not keep from giggling when everyone's stomach started growling. There is something about sitting in church on a Sunday morning that makes Baptists mighty hungry. We were thinking about the fried chicken, mashed potatoes and gravy waiting on us at home.

We enjoyed vacation bible school in the summer. It was only a week. We sang, did some crafts, had some cookies and juice and they told us what we thought were fairy tales. This was more fun than school. They did not scold us for being late and there were no tests, homework or report cards. No work at all. We liked that.

When we found ourselves in the theatre during one of the movies about the plight of Christians we would sit through it. But that was about it. These were the only movies that left us a little downcast. We did not ever mention re-enacting a movie about the Christians and the lions, Jesus on the cross, a sea opening up or umpteen million people wandering around on a desert for forty years.

These kinds of movies were just too creepy for us. We did not re-enact the Frankenstein or

Dracula movies either. Our instincts told us not to mess around with any of these kinds of movies.

Listening to the radio played a big part in enriching our lives. We would lie on the floor in a dark room and listen to Intersanctum or The Shadow. They tested our bravery and good won out in the end. The comedies were great. Our favorite was Baby Snooks.

Our radio noble heroes were The Lone Ranger and Sky King. We did not know anyone who flew their very own airplane before Sky King. So we thought he must know a lot that other people did not know. And he sent us the first thing from a radio show we could touch. For twenty-five cents and the lid liners from two jars of Peter Pan peanut butter he would send us an official Sky King ring. The likes of which we had never seen. We could wear it on our finger although it was very bulky. It contained a magnifying glass, a seal we could rub on paper to show our messages were official. The seal also glowed in the dark. This glow could be used to send secret signals. It also contained a ball point pen to write the messages with. It was the first ball point pen any of us had. We were not allowed any pens in the classroom yet and ball points were a new invention.

We cherished this ring. Tough got hers a week or so before the rest of us. We ooohed and aaahed. We could hardly wait and kept a close vigil on the mail. We were always enthusiastic about something. We always had something to look forward to.

The good movies and radio shows expanded our horizons and made our lives fuller than they would have been. The musicals were the glow from heaven that lit our universe. The comedies were one of the reasons we were such happy kids. According to Melody, the reason people were put on Earth was to make music. She constantly had us going around all the time singing songs from these delightful movies. While some of us spent a great deal of time imitating the comedians. Lou Costello was our favorite. These movies sent us on a journey we stayed on for the rest of our lives. Roy Rogers and Trigger kept us on the right trail.

We did not just want to be like Roy Rogers. We wanted to be Roy Rogers. And we believed we would always have a friend to save our seat in the grandest place a kid could be. The Saturday afternoon cowboy matinee.

THE COYOTE KIDS

The comic books we bought at the newsstand kept us well informed. They cost ten cents each and ranged from Lil' Lulu to Superman. We read them all. We never missed an issue. We swapped and traded them among ourselves every month until they were worn to a frazzle. Cowboy comic books were our favorite. Roy Rogers. Gene Autry.

To our surprise a really great new series emerged. It was in the Red Ryder and Little Beaver comic book. In one of the issues there sprang up a group of kids about our age. They were like a little posse that helped Red Ryder and his young side kick Little Beaver catch bad men.

Little Beaver already took our breath away in the movies. We were enthralled. He was an Indian boy with his own pinto pony. He had a bow and a quiver with real arrows in it. We loved him in the movies and we were captivated by the comic book.

When a young posse called The Coyote Kids was added to the scene we thought this was as good as life could possibly get. Thank you, Lord. The Coyote Kids were so popular they spun off from Red Ryder and had their own comic books. It was meant to be.

Right away we all knew we were the local version of the Coyote Kids. We were the most fascinating group of children there ever was or ever would be. We were the modern day Regulators. Although we had never heard of the Regulators of long ago.

Someone had to do it and we stepped up. Most everything on the crime scene had been very quiet during our life time. But, we figured if we were ever needed we would be there. We would be prepared.

Catching bad men was not the only thing The Coyote Kids did. We would volunteer in case of emergencies or anything that needed to be seen about or tended to... or regulated.

There were seven of us. If we had to name the one who inspired us the most it would have to be Melody. Barely eleven years old and already the brightest star. She got us started and kept us going. Always encouraging us to use our talents as much as possible through music, acting, costuming, staging.

We would get into character and stay in character - even at school. Sometimes we would be characters in a movie or we would be the movie actors themselves. We even wrote our notes to each other using the names of actors or roles they had played. And we were not limited by gender. When teachers would read one of these notes they were completely befuddled. Who is this note to? Who is it from? They never knew. John? John who? John Barrymore.

When we were at her house Melody would constantly change her clothes - or costumes - and come swaggering out into the living room. Boy costumes. Girl costumes. Always the actress. She was good at it. Real good and we could not get enough of her. Being with her was like being at a good movie.

Melody was tall for her age. Long legs. Dark hair to her shoulders. When she rode her pinto pony bare back she looked like an Indian princess. We could not see her as ever being anything other than a movie star. She shinned a bright light on us and would forever be our touchstone.

Each of The Coyote Kids raised the group to the top. The one person who took the group over the top was the one we called Tough. She enjoyed life to the fullest. She put everything into it and took everything out of it that it had to offer. And then some.

When we were wrestling she never said Uncle. She was the first person to ride her horse into the lake out to the dock and back. Did not think anything of it. Her horse did not give it a second thought either.

When Tough was only ten years old she went into the newspaper office, walked up to the publisher sitting at his desk and interviewed him about an upcoming baseball world series. It was a good interview. She took notes thanked him and left. Fearless.

Tough and Melody were equally as fearless and brave. They were not afraid of anything. Sometimes the three of us would crawl out of Melody's bedroom window in the middle of the night and sneak down to the lake. We could have just gone out the front door. It would have been easier. But it would not have been as much fun. Knowing them made me braver than I would have been.

Tough would struggle and always come out on top and win. She enjoyed being the center of attention. This was good because most of the time she was the center of attention. Melody and Tough and I took turns being the stars while the others would be our audience. We were very fascinated with each other. But, all in all, Tough was the fire that boiled the pot.

The boy we called Else was one of us although he was often way out along the edge. Somewhere else. If we needed any of his specialties he would always deliver. One time we were going to have a knife throwing contest but we did not have any knives that were good for throwing. So we called on Else. The next day he showed up with two dozen ice picks from his grandfather's ice plant.

Once we got the hang of it we would throw the picks at a target on a board. They would spin once then stick in point first. We got pretty accurate right away. Else could come up with just about anything-make anything possible. That is, when he was around.

If we or his family had not seen him for a few days we knew where he was. We would saddle up some horses and bicycles and head to the river. And there he would be. Camping out near a hollow tree. If it rained he would sit inside the tree. Or just let the rain on him. A sack of food, a camp fire, a B-B gun. Who could blame him for wanting to be there. At the river. Under the trees. The ground was completely shaded.

This was a very old Indian spot for fishing. Down stream there were some large stones lined up in the shape of a V. The water was shallow. About two or three feet deep- white sand. He could herd the fish into the V then grab them with his hands. Else was attracted to this place like a magnet.

Way out in the pasture between the river and the hard road was a small frame house. Plain and kind of run down. Seems like no one lived there. We had never thought much about it all the times we had traveled about a hundred yards passed it. While we were down by the river at Else's camp we heard a really loud explosion. An earth shaking boom. We figured the phosphate mines were dynamiting. Although it sounded closer than the mines were. Oh, well.

On the way back to town we were amazed with hysterical laughter. The little house was only half there. Some of the walls were still standing but the roof and the attic were completely gone.

We did not see a scrape of them anywhere. They were plum gone.

Someone had a still in the attic. The heat from the contraption caused a Hiroshima type blast like the one we saw in the newsreel at the movies. Smaller but similar. Fortunately no one was in the house when it blew up. If there was, no one ever found him.

Loren said, there was too much sunshine on the moonshine.

Loren was always smiling and joking. His hair was the color of a hay stack. His big toothy grin shinned on us like the sun. Loren loved everything in life and everything in life loved him. He was as smart as Einstein but he still loved to play cowboys with his stick horse and his cap pistol. He was the child every parent wish they could have. He was indulged by a wealthy grandmother and aunts but he was the kind of child no one could spoil no matter how hard someone tried to spoil him. He was always kind, thoughtful and generous. He had everything. From cowboy boots to bicycles. And he made sure he shared everything with everyone.

Although Loren was very small for his age he was a very big person to us. He was always inventing some kind of gadgets and they almost always worked. He had the first crystal radio we had ever seen. He put it together and strung a wire antenna on his roof. He had a big short wave radio we listened to. He said he would be able to talk on it in a few years. Talk to other people. Wow.

This little guy knew everything about science. He told us about the speed of light. He told us about a lot of things. Sometimes we did not know what in the heck he was talking about. He always told funny stories about himself and the things he was trying to invent. We admired him.

The odds told us it was impossible for two kids as smart as Loren and Two Pound to wind up in the small little group in such a tiny town as Sterling. But they did.

Two-Pound was so sickly she did not even go to school for the first three years. Her parents taught her at home. And taught her they did. She learned a lot on her own from books and magazines. She had her own microscope and telescope. She said she wanted to see it all. Her father taught her arithmetic and science and how to play a trumpet. Her mother taught her about English and reading and writing and maybe some history and stuff.

Her mother was a really good piano player. Self taught. Played by ear. That house was busting with music. Two Pound is okay now. Very small for her age but okay. She and Loren were both very small. Tiny.

One time at Two-Pound and Melody's house Two Pound and Loren were sitting on the floor leaning against the wall. They were talking and writing and drawing. We were watching them. Then they informed us that the only way we could ever get to the moon was to build a rocket ship that was in three stages. As the fuel was used up in the first stage it would drop off. Then when the fuel was used up in the second stage it would drop off. This would lighten the load tremendously. The third stage would get us to the moon. We would land gently by going down back end first and slowly reducing the rocket thrust.

We asked them how would we get back. They said, With a big thrust and then gravity would bring us back to Earth and we would land with a parachute. Probably in the ocean.

We just sat and stared at them for a while like we usually would do. Then we told them that someday they would be writers and make space man movies like Buck Rogers and Flash Gorden.

We thought they would be the best science fiction writers there ever was or ever would be.

Although, deep in our hearts, we knew that if anyone could get The Coyote Kids to the moon and back it would be Loren and Two-Pound.

Slip, our very own private detective, knew everything about everyone. He knew everyones name, where they lived, where they worked, what kind of car they drove, their license tag number. His mother worked at the court house. Every time some one did some business at her office she would come home and talk about it to who ever might be around. Slip would listen and take notes.

He had a little note book he held in the palm of his hand that he wrote in with a tiny little pencil. It was the kind that looked like a bullet. Pull it apart turn it around, stick it back together and it was long enough to write with. He was quiet, observant and dark. Kids would some times steer clear of him because they thought he was taking names of kids to report to the teacher for some kind of bad behavior. He probably was just writing down what brand of jeans they were wearing.

Slip got Loren to make him a little crystal radio with a wire antennae and a small ear phone that clipped over his head. He would get in a corner somewhere and listen. He looked like a Nazi spy or something. Sometimes he wore the little radio on his wrist. Like Dick Tracy.

Slip and an older neighbor kid who had a paper route would scan the big Tampa paper, among others, and cut out any unusual or mystifying articles that had anything to do with crime. They had a couple of scrap books full of pasted in articles of unsolved crimes- or crimes they did not think were resolved to suit their standards.

This may have seemed like a game to some people but it would come in mighty handy when the time came the Coyote Kids would help solve the worst crime that ever happened in Sterling.

And, then there was me. They called me Charley. My family named me after Charlie Chaplin. One of the most famous people in the world. People loved him. Really loved him. He was one of the movie stars that got people through the great depression. The little Tramp. The little Clown. He made movies and the whole world better than it would have been without him.

Part of me was Charlie. I was a clown. I would do anything for a laugh. I was full of mischief. The kind that gets kids into trouble. But it never did me. If you heard someone shoot off a firecracker during the Star Spangled Banner at the football game it was me. Melody and Tough would laugh until they hurt.

I was also apart of each of my precious friends. Part of me was a detective like Slip. I was not as smart as Loren and Two-Pound but I was as hammy and stage struck as Melody. We were both very good at acting. She could sing a lot better than I could but I could sing pretty good too. I was brave but not as brave as Tough. When we were all together we could turn the town on its ear.

And, sometimes, quite often, I liked to wander around by myself. All alone. To see what I could see. And to see what I could hear. And to see what I could feel. To see just what all was out there. To walk around in silence. To watch and listen and feel and learn. And to never forget what I saw and heard and felt and learned.

Since I was a little bit of each of us I kept the communication going among the group. I was the glue that held us together. This was almost impossible to do because we were seven extremely strong individual ten year old personalities.

It was a ritual that actually sized us up. We cut our fingers and pressed them together so the blood would run together. We were blood brothers and sisters. Just like the Indians in the movies. This was Melody's and Tough's idea. I was able to get up the courage to do this because I was doing it with them.

I was with Loren more often than the others because we were neighbors in town. Melody, Two-Pound, Slip and Tough lived in a phosphate village a few miles west of town. Oakridge. Sometimes they came into town on week-ends. Or we went out there. Else lived in town. We saw him when we saw him. Sometimes often. Sometimes not so often.

The closeness I had with Loren grew to be so deep it was beyond us. Last Christmas morning I walked out on the back porch. My family lived in an upstairs apartment in a wood frame building. The porch was open air with railings like the balconies in cowboy movies.

I had just strapped on my new cap pistol and holster. What a beauty. The pistol looked real. It shot caps on around paper disc rather than the paper tape kind. The holster and belt were white suede leather with white flannel backing.

I was headed to Loren's house to show him my new six shooter as fast as I could get there.

Just as I got to the top of the stairs there was Loren. Maybe fifteen feet from the bottom of the stairs. He was wearing a new pair of six shooters just like Roy Rogers. He drew and fired at me. I drew and fired back. We both got off six shots. I grabbed my chest and pretended to stumble halfway down the stairs - I flipped over the hand rail and landed flat on my back on the soft deep sand on the driveway.

This spontaneous communication welded our hearts together forever with out a word having been spoken.

The most amazing and mysterious experience I ever had was with Loren.

There were some mined out areas south of town only about fifteen blocks from downtown. This is where the mining company bad dug up the phosphate and left the ground looking like something from another planet. There were great dirt dunes and huge holes. The holes filled up with water and made dozens of lakes. We would climb up on the dunes and look around and marvel. Some of the holes had been filled in with dirt and were flat and wind blown almost smooth but had tiny ripples like on a wash board. We could see the flats only by climbing on the dunes. We called all this The Pits. Short for the Phosphate Pits. Compared to being in town this was as different as night and day. There were no shade trees out there. They dug them all up. All this was as spooky and as wonderful as walking on the moon.

It was not unusual for a group of kids out cruising around on bikes or horses - or walking when someone would call out. "LET'S GO TO THE PITS!"

On this day it had just been Loren and me. We rode our bikes down the abandoned dirt road a lot further than we had ever been before.

Sometimes people would fish in the lakes. No one else was around that day. We were more alone than we had ever been. Somehow this day seemed different. Good but different. We came to a place we had never been before. It was a tower built of old grey unpainted boards. A good two stories high. There were four big corner posts and horizontal braces and cross braces that made big Xs in between. There were no stairs.

Neither of us said a word. Loren just started climbing the tower with me right behind him. He would put his foot on a horizontal brace then somehow put his other foot on a cross brace. As he moved up I was one step behind him putting my foot where his foot had just been a second earlier and holding on with my hands.

On top of the tower was a room. Maybe ten feet by ten feet. There was an opening where we came in and a couple of open air windows. Must have been a office of some kind. Or a look out place to watch the work going on down below. There must have been some stairs at some time. The workers would not have wanted to climb up and down those beams all day every day. But there were no stairs or a ladder on that day.

Loren and I had climbed up those beams as easy and as fast as little bugs running up a wall. We were as light as feathers. It was like a stream of wind - on this perfectly still day - had lifted us up by our jeans and put us there in that little room with absolutely no effort on our part.

There was nothing in that room except a piece of white cloth on the floor. When we looked closer we saw it was a dirty baby diaper. How in the world could anyone climb up there carrying a baby. And why would they. Did some people spend the night up there. There must have been some stairs long ago. That dirty baby diaper had been there a long time. But how long. Why would anyone come up here with a baby even if there had been some stairs. The only way up there was the way we came up. There were no stairs. We looked.

Going back down was as easy as climbing up. It was easier than going up and down a carpeted stair case in one of the many two story houses in Sterling.

A couple of months later I was out riding my bike and I went to the farm that was the last buildings before leaving the paved road and going down the dirt road that led to The Pits. A nice lady lived at the farm and would let me and The Girl who loved horses so much ride the pony that lived at the farm.

No one was at home that day so I mounted my bike and struck out somewhere else. But where. Then it rang in my head, Go to The Pits!

I was all alone. My ten year old judgment was no judgment at all. The Pits were as remote as remote as can be. If something happened to a lone kid down there it was no telling when they would find them. Very few, if any, parents had ever been down there and probably did not know the pits were there. So they did not know we went down there. Regularly.

I went straight to the tower. Put my foot on the first rung. And that was it. I could go no further. I was not scared. I was not afraid of being alone. I did not think about being alone. I wanted to climb the tower. But I could not. I had gone up the tower before like I was being dragged up in Loren's draft. Without him climbing up ahead of me I could not climb one inch. I felt as though I weighed a ton. I could not figure where to put my foot next. No matter how hard I tried I could not get off the ground. Was it because Loren was not there for me to follow? I do not know.

I did not ever tell anyone about my lone experience at the tower. Not even Loren. We did not tell anyone about climbing the tower and the dirty baby diaper. Our climb was successful but it had been a very strange day. We never talked about it to each other either. Something had lifted us up that day. It was as if Loren was a magnet pulling me up behind him. Something lifted him up too. It was if we were both weightless.

We continued to go to The Pits as usual. But we never went way down the long back road. We never went back to the tower.

We were children - very young. Still like babies in some ways. Yet we were doing things for beyond anything most adults were likely to do. The courage and inspiration to experience these adventures can be contributed to the culture of the times and the culture that Sterling created for us.

We led a charmed life. In return we sprinkled our star dust that nourished an enchanted town.

WALK WITH THE GIRL

Sterling was an enchanted little town whose kids could go out their door - walk in any direction and experience an amount of pleasure that was amazing beyond amazement. This is what we did. Regularly.

The Girl Who Loved Horses So Much lived in an apartment building behind mine and down one half a block. Quite often we would walk the ten blocks south to the farm where the lady would let us ride the brown pony that lived there. The walk was as great as getting there.

The address on my building was 505. That meant there were only four short city blocks to Main Street. We would walk one block south to a wooden fenced-in horse lot where a very pleasant, beautiful white welsh pony lived. The purpose of these walks was to pet the horses, talk to them, listen to them, pull grass along the fence they could not reach and feed it to them. One block east, just beyond our elementary school was another horse lot.

We had seven or eight stops to make along the way. We would visit with ten or twelve horses. This was all within the city limits. It took quite a while to get to the farm what with all the corral calls we had to make.

We walked along the street that was one of the oldest in town. The houses along the way were ancient. At least they were ancient to us. Almost all of them were large two story houses with porches all around. Some of them even had porches upstairs. We imagined there were good cowboys on those upstairs balconies watching over us. Most of the streets in Sterling were lined with giant oak trees. We had plenty of shade. Tree branches met over the streets to make a canopy.

The story about one of the streets was that back in the 1800's when the dirt street was first cut through it was used as a race track for horses. It was lined limb touching limb - canopied and shady. People stood along the sides of the dusty street in the shade. There were also a few wooden bleachers. A day at the races. Horses were the stars in Sterling from the very beginning - and still were.

The farm was covered with more than forty acres of stuff for us to love. We loved the barn, the hay loft, the hay. We loved anything that even remotely had anything to do with horses. There were chickens pecking around, even turkeys. There was a dog or two. I do not know how many cats. Ducks in a small pond. We got buckets of feed and fed everything as soon as we got there.

We marveled at the hitching posts, water troughs, leather tack, old saddles, plows. Everything that may have been on a farm was there. Anything that came to a farm never left. It stayed forever. Animals would come and go but everything else stayed. We would walk way far out in the pasture. This is where I learned that even though cows are very large they only make a tiny narrow trail when they walk. I never could figure that out.

There was a creek that ran through the thick woods beyond the cow pasture. We were sure the creek was magic and did not question it. We were also certain the woods continued on forever and ever and never ended. We believed there was nothing beyond the woods except more and more woods. The Girl said so. I believed her. We felt the same way about the movie screen at the theatre. For us there was nothing beyond that screen except an infinite distance of more and more of what we saw on our side of the screen.

We never knew how much time we spent at the farm. We were not on any clock anywhere. We were somewhere outside of time. We picked wild flowers and tossed them into the stream - sat and watched them drift slowly away. The Girl said the flowers were going way far away - a distance no one would ever see. But that was okay because we were the ones who sent the flowers. We walked the cows' long narrow trail. We put one foot directly in front of the other like the cows did. We were a cow. She was the front I was the back. Eventually, when we took turns riding the pony back to the barn the cows would always walk with us in a line along their narrow path. For us, that was an official round-up, the same as any other. Just like in the movies.

Before we left we would always curry the pony. We brushed him from top to bottom - from side to side. We combed his tail and his mane. He just stood there. He thanked us with a soft whinney.

We had walked to the farm. When we traveled back to our homes we did not walk. We floated.

The Girl was very much like us yet very different. She was our age-ten-but was much more mature - sophisticated. An only child. She and her parents came here from somewhere in New York. We were all very Southern. She talked a little different from us but not fast like some Yankees.

The Girl had poise. Her posture was smooth and fluid. She was tall, slender. Hair down to her shoulders that looked like it had been poured out of a jar of honey. She looked like an adult movie star - but very young.

We all knew she had brought something special to us even though we did not know exactly what that "something special" was. After a little over a year she and her parents moved to a large city.

How ironic it was that someone who loved horses so much would come from so far away to land in Sterling - the horse town - for one fine year. She was a clear example of the right person coming to the right place at the right time to mix and match her magic with the magic of Sterling.

She was not a Coyote Kid. She had not been here long enough. She came here... sprinkled her star dust... then she was gone... like the flowers in the stream. She left her glow. It is still glowing.

We felt a tremendous loss when she left. This was the first time we had felt the pain of loosing a playmate we were so fond of. We thought this would be the only time. But... it would not be...

THE GREAT WALK

I woke up this morning to the sound of a rooster crowing. That was one of the best things about living in Sterling. No matter where you woke up you could always hear a rooster crowing. Most of the houses had at one time or another what they called a chicken yard. They were fenced in with chicken wire and had a wooden homemade hen house. Inside the little houses were shelves sectioned off into nests for the hens to lay eggs. The nests were lined with pine needles or hay. This was cozy and worked out real well. Except for one time.

A widow woman we called Miss Birdie was trying to figure out a way to make some money. She decided to raise chickens. So she bought twenty hens and twenty roosters. She never had any chickens of her own so she did not know any better. My father said she must have thought she was going to marry them off into pairs. What a mess. There was such a ruckus. The neighbors went in there and took out all the roosters. They told Miss Birdie to just sell the eggs.

This was the first day of Christmas vacation. What a nice change of pace. This was the two weeks that always stood alone. On its own.

The only thing I loved more than wandering around Sterling with my friends was wandering around Sterling all by myself. Being by myself made time longer. I could see more and hear more and feel more. And more of it would sink into me and stay there forever.

When I left my building it was chilly. Almost cold. It was hazy. It was not exactly raining but I could feel tiny specks of cold mist sting my cheeks. I could not see it but I could feel it. I was wearing my trench coat and a little hat with the brim turned down. I looked like someone in a Humphrey Bogart movie.

On my great walk, the first place I always went was down to the white pony's corral at the end of the block. She could see me coming and would trot to the fence and whinnie. After feeding her breakfast of a carrot and half an apple (I ate the other half) I dared to strike out to the ice house and to the cemetery.

The ice house was owned by Else's family. Sometimes he was there and sometimes he was not. If he was there we would go inside and look around. The inside of an ice house looks entirely different than any other place. There is nothing that is even similar. He showed me how the walls were about two feet thick and hollow. They were filled with saw dust to insulate and to keep the ice frozen. The insides were mostly made of wood. Huge - and I mean huge - beams. Up and down and back and forth. It was dark in there and it seemed as old as time.

It was fascinating in there and at the same time really creepy. There were moaning sounds. Else said it was ghosts. The ice house had been there for a very long time. Someone died inside there. He is still there. Can not see him but he is there. Else says he is a friend.

The ice house was much more fun in the summer time. Loren and I would walk down to the ice house pulling his little red wagon. For twenty cents we would get twenty five pounds of crushed ice. Pull it home. Put on our bathing suits and play in the ice all afternoon. We would rub it on us. Sling the water off chunks of it onto each other. Fill a wash tub with water and ice and stand in it. Take a pot and dip the icy cold water over our heads and feel the joy of that iciness run down our bodies. Even on the hottest day by the time the sun started to go down we were not hot at all. We were very cool.

The cemetery was only a couple of blocks down a dirt road from the ice house. The oldest part with the ancient graves was the most interesting. Slipping down to the cemetery after dark was a rite of passage for kids. Anyone who was anyone had been to the cemetery at night before they were fourteen years old. Parents did not know about this.

The night I went was with Tough, Else, Loren and Melody and a couple of kids from my neighborhood. It was near Halloween. The moon was full and had red streaks on it. Tough kept chanting, Blood on the moon. The dead shall rise at nine.

We all got so scared we started running and kept running for about a mile. Except for Else. He just stayed there and hung around. We were glad this was something we only had to do once.

It is remarkable how much different a cemetery looks in the daytime and how it looks at night

During the day it is like walking through a big bedroom where everyone is sleeping.

The old man was here today. He usually was. He comes here regularly and picks up moss and branches and keeps the place nice and neat. Sometimes he rakes a little and cleans the mildew off the tombstones.

He always wore a grey suit. It looked like some kind of uniform. He said he knew all the people buried in this old cemetery. I never did do the math so I believed him.

General Sterling was buried there. So were several other Confederate soldiers. Their graves had special markers on them. The old man kept the Confederate graves looking like brand new. He told us the reason the Confederate soldiers' tombstones were pointed at the top rather than flat was so Yankee soldiers could not sit on them. He also said cemeteries are not for the dead. They are for the living. Else told us the old man was from some time other than now. This is something only Else would know.

I was covering a lot of ground today. Good. Next stop was Sarge's place. He was a hero in the war. Got wounded. Not too bad. He said his jeep, Nellie Belle, saved his life. When he was in

Germany the jeep had a machine gun mounted on the back. One day when he and two other soldiers were fixing to get killed they jumped into the jeep and plowed their way through a bunch of Nazi soldiers. Sarge was driving. Another soldier was firing away with the machine gun. The third one had a Tommy gun and was mowing them down too. The jeep rolled over hill and dell, ditches and streams. They would not have made it without Nellie Belle. He brought the jeep home with him. It is out in the yard today with him working on it. He loved the jeep.

He loved his dog too. Her name was Gypsey. She was a hero too. She carried messages from one group of soldiers to another. She had a slight wound. They gave her a Purple Heart. They also made her some Sergeant stripes she was wearing when she came home. They fastened them on her front leg with elastic. She was a German Shepherd dog. Don't know why they called her German. Those were the people she helped whip. This town was crammed full of heroes.

Sarge's house was a great place to hang around. Sit in the jeep. Play with Gypsey. In the summer time Sarge grew and sold delicious tomatoes in his back yard. He charged about fifteen cents a pound. There was a bench and a scale back there. People would weigh their tomatoes and leave the money in a coffee can. Honor system.

Gypsey was not here today. She was out on her route. Every morning she would walk toward the post office and meet the mail man for that neighborhood. He wore a uniform and carried the mail in a big leather pouch. Gypsey would walk along with him for the whole route. She was still delivering messages. It took two or three hours. Then she would walk home. Somehow she could tell the difference between work days and holidays and Sundays. We do not know how she could tell the difference but she could. If it was not a work day she just stayed home.

Sarge's house was not very far from my elementary school and the big theatre next to it. I could see there was a car by the back door. The door was half open. There was someone there today. Turns out they were going to rehearse for some kind of Christmas program. Some of the churches.

I stood just inside the door and looked in. There was a little bit of light in there. Not much but enough I could see a girl on the stage. She was looking up at the balcony. This was the same girl who sang the lead in the four high school operettas we had watched right here. I saw up in the balcony the boy who had sung the other lead in the operettas. They were the only people in the theatre. They had both graduated last June. Went to college. Back home for the Christmas holidays. We could not imagine they would ever be married to anyone other than each other. It seemed like they had been married to each other their whole lives.

Then the next thing I knew the boy started singing, The Indian Love Song. This was the song they sang in the operetta, Rose Marie, last spring. I'll be loving you... oooo-ooo-ooo-ooh. They sang back and forth to each other. They sang the whole song. Just the two of them. No piano or anything. The sound had me spellbound. Their perfect voices in that perfect sounding theatre in the dim light. One on the stage. The other in the balcony. My scalp tingled and up and down my back. When they finished singing I was not able to enter the building and I was not able to turn and walk away. Hearing them sing into this empty theatre was even a million times better than when I heard them last spring when the theatre was filled with fidgety, shuffling children.

I could not move. I went down on one knee and crab walked backward. I did not want them to see me. It did not seem right for me to see and hear what I just saw and heard. It was too private. In my zany ten year old judgment I thought they would not be able to see me if I crawled backward. It worked. They did not see me. And I knew I would never see or hear anything like that again. It was another one of those moments in Sterling that could never be duplicated.

For the next couple of hours I wandered around downtown. Browsed through both dime stores and both hardware stores. Went to the music store and bought a recording of Doris Day singing, It's Magic. This would be Melody's Christmas present. It cost seventy-nine cents. We all loved this song. Magic seemed to describe Sterling and The Coyote Kids.

I stopped and watched a grown man standing on the side walk in front of his radio shop twirling the propeller on a rubber band powered model airplane. He was surrounded by kids. When it was cranked up as tight as it would go he pushed it into the air. It flew high and wide. Went over the top of his building and landed somewhere in the yard of the hotel.

By this time I was working up an appetite so I started looking around for Loren. Melody, Tough and Two-Pound were doing a dance up and down the court house steps. The big concrete porch made a perfectly good stage. I thought I could see Slip hiding in the bushes keeping an eye on everything.

I could tell there was a lot going on at the court house so I figured Loren might be inside getting an eyeful. I went to look for him.

There had been a big trial about some moonshiners. They had gotten convicted. Now the deputy sheriffs were carrying out the evidence and pouring it down the storm drains. The evidence was the moonshine. Some of it was in big metal five gallon cans. Some of it was in big glass jugs. Just as I saw Loran coming towards me in the hallway a man carrying two glass jugs turned the corner too sharp. He slipped a little and one of those dang jugs hit the corner of the wall. It was made of hard tile. The jug broke to smithereens and spilled on Loren's shoes and the cuff of his pants. He sure smelled awful for such a little boy.

Outside there were umpteen empty containers and the deputies were still pouring the stuff down the storm drains. This was not smart at all. It was unbelievably dumb. It had not rained in a while. Not enough to rinse the drains. The moonshine they were pouring was just sitting there in the dry tunnels. It moved a little but just enough to go from one corner drain to the next. The whole town reeked of moonshine. The odor was coming up from each storm drain opening. Everyone could have gotten drunk from the fumes. Lord have mercy.

Loren was hungry too so we went by Melody's theatre to get them to go eat at the drug store on the corner.

Tough was doing her impersonation of Betty Hutton. Singing and dancing the song, Doctor, Lawyer and Indian Chief. She had it nailed. People were watching her. We all agreed Betty Hutton was without a doubt the most talented, unique, dazzling actress, singer, dancer, comedienne there ever was.

The drug store on the corner was a story book setting. For years there had been an elderly man sitting at a push cart just outside the front door. His cart was shaped like a big wooden box on wheels with sliding doors on top. Inside there were knick-knacks and novelties. We did not know if he sold much of this stuff. Most people did not know what was inside the cart. One day I asked what was inside so he opened it. Odds and ends - bracelets - whistles - tiny plastic animals. I bought a little box that was labeled, Mexican Jumping Beans. They were not real. They were just little capsules with a B-B inside that would fly up on one end if you rolled them around.

Almost everything he sold was newspapers. And he sure sold a lot of them. He sold the big city morning paper in the morning and the big city afternoon paper in the afternoon. They cost ten cents. He would hold all his coins in his mostly paralyzed hand until he had enough for a dollar. Then he would ask someone to take the coins inside the drugstore and exchange them for a dollar bill. He would wad the bill into a little ball and stuff it in his pocket. I did this for him every day I was downtown. There was always someone to bring him lunch.

The chair he sat on was from inside the drugstore. Someone would bring it out to him every morning. The cart was kept inside the drugstore over night. One of the owners of the men's clothing store next door drove him home to his tiny house every evening. He drove him back to town the next morning.

The man could not walk very well and it was difficult to make out what he was saying. Some people said he had been a medic and had been wounded in WWI and that was why he could not walk or talk too good. But he was there on his corner every morning except Sunday. He and Gypsy took the day off.

There he sat at his cart on the days after WWII when all the soldiers who had just come home were standing around on his corner. He was surrounded by heroes. And he was a hero too.

Some people said he had a stroke that made him frail. But we liked to believe he was wounded in the long ago war. Either way he was a hero to us. His name was Doc.

We got to the drugstore just in time. The man who owned the drugstore, Mr. Pillsbury, was taking his lunch break and was telling his stories to people sitting at the little round tables and in the booths. Tough asked, What in the heck is that I smell?! We told her Loren's shoes had been drinking and the deputies were pouring moonshine down the storm drains. We had a really good, long laugh. Everyone laughed with us.

The people who enjoyed their jobs the most were the people who worked at this drug store.

We over heard one of the girls who worked the soda fountain say that every morning she would crave to get to work. She would sit in a chair and wait for the time for the drugstore to open. They had fun. They would make bets as to which one of the girls who worked at the beauty parlor would leave the most lipstick on her coffee cup.

The drugstore had seemed like an even more happy place for the last month or two. There was a new tonic on the market. No prescription needed. People could buy it off the shelf or pay a little extra and the girls at the fountain would put some in their milk shake. This was a Hadacol milk shake. Very popular. Today Loren ordered his first and last Hadacol milk shake. The tonic had alcohol in it. There we sat with our delicious twenty-five cent sandwiches and our delicious ten cent cherry cokes. There sat Loren with his delicious thirty cent milk shake rosy cheeked. He already reeked of booze. Now he was getting loaded. This was an unusual day. Even for Sterling.

The milk shakes were served in a tall glass. The girls would leave the metal container it was mixed in on the table. Most people did not drink all the shake that was in the metal container. The girls saved what was left and drank it themselves after they took the leftovers back behind the counter.

The owner's wife, Mrs. Pillsbury, came up to the counter and asked one of the girls, Where are our cokes? She was supposed to bring some cokes to the people who worked in the back of the store in the pharmacy. The girl gave a blank stare and said, Cokes? What cokes? She was not exactly sober.

Pretty soon after that the owners of the drugstore decided to stop selling Hadacol milkshakes. It had started to get a little weird around there sometimes.

So here we sat. Me, Melody, Two-Pound, Loren and Tough, as Mr. Pillsbury walked to the center of the tables and started telling one of his great stories. He always looked like he was talking to just one table of people but he knew we could all hear him.

Our favorite story had been the one where his grandfather, a doctor, was crossing the river in his horse and buggy. The doctor looked up and there on horse back were two scraggly men on the other bank with guns in their hands. At that same moment four arrows shot from bows went into the chests of the two bandits. Two each. Mr. Pillsbury said the bandits were leftovers from the Civil War. They were probably addicted to morphine and figured the doctor had some in his satchel. They would have killed the doctor if it had not been for the four sure shot Indians.

The Indian who looked like the chief or the straw-boss or something said, You heap good medicine man. We no let bad men hurt you. Then they rode away.

Today's story topped them all. Mr. Pillsbury said a few months ago a big Army truck full of soldiers pulled up outside and parked. Took up two spaces. An officer came inside to get the soldiers a whole bunch of cold drinks, crackers, cookies and stuff.

The officer told Mr. Pillsbury that they had been sent a mile or two from here to a place called The Pits. Someone had seen something land out there. Then later it took off and disappeared. It came straight down then went straight up. There were four big pod impressions on the ground. These were what the air craft had landed on. The ground looked like it had been incinerated. The sand looked like glass.

The location was only about a quarter of a mile from where Loran and I had floated up the wooden tower. The best we could figure it was about that same time, too.

Loren and I looked at each other with all four of our eye brows raised as far as they could go. Then he got a serious look on his face and said, Dang! They got down here before we could get up there. Two Pound said, Very interesting. Melody said, This would make a great musical. Tough said, I wish we could have been there. Maybe we could have captured them.

Melody had called a rehearsal for two-o'clock. Time to go. Just as we were about to leave, a little kid carrying a note came in and asked for me. He said a guy named Slip said to give the note to me and I would give him a dime. So I did. The note said that the people from the pound were coming to get the Mama cat and her four kittens that had been living at the court house in the bushes.

We all ran to the general area where we had last seen the Mama cat and kittens. Melody said, We will distract the people from the pound. And her troupe did exactly that. They were singing, Coming Around the Mountain. This gave Loren and me time to find all the kitties. We followed the sound of the meowing and mewing. They were in a stair well that went to the basement. The Mama was trapped inside a cage and the kittens were trying to get to her. This was so sad to see. Loren and I went into a rage and became super strong.

Loren opened the cage and put one kitten inside with the Mama. He picked up the cage and ran as fast as a bat out of Hades. I could only see kittens' numbers two and three. Where was number four? I picked up the two kittens, put them inside my trench coat and ran as fast as I could.

There I was following in Loren's draft again. I figured he was headed to his house. We had about five blocks to go. Right away I heard a third set of foot steps behind me. I though it was the ugly man from the pound. I did not look back. I could not bear the thought. I was already in pain. It felt like the kittens had two hundred claws and they were all sticking in my stomach and my chest.

Loran and I kept running until we came to an old abandoned chicken yard behind his house. This was when we realized the third set of footsteps was Else. Where in the heck did he come from? He was carrying kitten number four.

The kitties would be safe in the hen house. It was fenced in. We took an old quilt and made kitty nests out of the hens' nests. We got them some food, milk and water. In a few months they would be going to horse barns and earn their keep by chasing the mice away from the feed.

It was amazing how fast Loren had sobered up. Even so, he still stank. He just told his parents about the jug of moonshine that spilled on his shoes. Our parents never knew what to expect next.

As I was lying in my cozy warm bed that night I thought: Today's great walk ended up with a great run. I smiled for a long time in the darkness. Watching happy movies on the back of my eyelids. Once again The Coyote Kids ruled.

Little did I know that Spring would greet us with the harshest lesson we would ever have to learn: When a town as good as Sterling experiences something really bad it hurts worse than it would have in a bad town.

We were not prepared for what was coming up. But we would get through it by drawing on the strength of the culture and the atmosphere the town of Sterling had long since created for us. The people, place and times served us well as did our heroes from beyond the silver screen. Roy Rogers gave us The Code of the West. Betty Hutton gave us Chutzpah.

MIZ LERNER

We could not imagine children growing up anywhere other than in Sterling. And we certainly could not imagine children going through elementary school without having Miz Lerner for a teacher.

One school year with her changed our lives forever. We were entirely different people at the end of the year than we were at the beginning. We became worldly.

Miz Lerner had such a love and deep passion for teaching it was rather hard to believe. She told most everyone that if the school did not pay her she would teach for free. And she would be willing to pay them to let her teach. In over twenty years she had not missed work a single day.

Other classes took place in the class room, the auditorium, the play ground or maybe an occasional field trip to the fire station or somewhere. Miz Lerner's class took place all over the world.

Her father was a doctor. He loved to travel as much as his daughter loved to teach. They spent summers traveling all over the world. They would have gone to other planets if there had been a boat or train to take them there.

Miz Lerner inherited her father's love for traveling. Now she had two passions. Traveling and teaching and Boy! These two things went together mighty good. Everyday she told us a story about somewhere she had been as a child or as an adult. In the summers she worked as a travel guide that escorted groups all over the world.

She had a gadget we had never seen before. It was a "View Master". It was for looking at pictures. There were little squares of film on a disc. We put the disc into the contraption and held it up to the light. And, behold! We could see Egypt, China, France or England or anywhere else. The picture of Grand Canyon took my breath away. Each disc was a different country. Each square of film was a different scene. We could change the scenes by pushing down on a lever.

Together with these and other pictures she showed us, coupled with her endless stories, she took us all over the world on a magic carpet we flew around on for the rest of our lives.

Many of the children in her classes were from very modest homes where there was little or no outside communications. Some had never been more than a very few miles from town. Miz Lerner knew this. She was determined to open their eyes and expand their world. She succeeded.

She never raised her voice. Always spoke in the same low, distinct southern tone. Always walked with the same gait. Never sped up. Never slowed down. She only had one destination: TO TEACH!

This was a very orderly class. There wasn't much shuffling or jabbering. That was because Miz Lerner demanded attention and kept us spellbound with her amazing stories. The one we would never forget was when she was at the pyramids in Egypt. A little boy about our age said to her that if she gave him fifty cents he would climb to the top of the pyramid. She said she would give him fifty cents but he was not to climb the pyramid. It was dangerous and he might get hurt. She gave him the fifty cents. She then went around the corner to take a look at the Rosetta Stone. This was a big flat top rock. A long, long time ago when people first got ready to write stuff down they scratched it on top of this rock. Don't know why they named it Rosetta.

When she came back around to where the boy had been there was a crowd gathered at the base of the pyramid. The boy had climbed for his next customer and had fallen. He was dead. There was a good lesson in this. There was always a good lesson in her stories.

We were very glad Miz Lerner also had a passion and a talent for music. We did a lot of singing in that room. We had music books, a pitch pipe and a record player.

We sang several different songs each week. We always sang Miz Lerner's favorites. "I'm Forever Blowing Bubbles" and "Now is the Hour". She said she sang the one about blowing bubbles when she was a little girl. She blew beautiful bubbles. They floated around and even went way up into the clouds. And kept going forever. The "Beautiful Bubbles Forever" described Miz Lerner.

"Now is the Hour" is the best good-bye song there ever was. It is a song that says we know you have to leave now. But we will always think about you. And we hope you will always think about us. We believe you will comeback some day. When you do we will be right here waiting for you.

It seems like these two songs were written for Miz Lerner and for this year's class.

In other classes we were told to sit down and shut up. Miz Lerner told us to stand up and sing or tell a story. This was the first time Melody sang in front of an audience. We had a hard time getting her up there and sing. Once she heard our applause we could not get her to sit down. She sang "Manana". She knew all the words and was on key. That was Melody's beginning.

When Miz Singum was rehearsing the operettas at night Miz Lerner was always there to help. She knew what she loved and kept at it.

Don't think that Miz Lerner was all arts and music. She was excellent at teaching arithmetic and all the other stuff too. She had a way of making it easy to learn. She made us feel we were a part of what we were learning. Miz Lerner loved to teach, to travel, to learn and to come back and teach some more.

One of the best things that ever happened to us was that every day after lunch Miz Lerner would read to us. This was heaven. She came up with the best dang books we had ever heard of and she did not test us on what she read to us.

The best book was about a girl our age who lived and worked on a strawberry farm only about thirty or forty miles from Sterling. She was smart and she was brave. One time she saw that a mean boy had put a baby bunny rabbit in a cage with a sleeping rattle snake for the snake to eat when he woke up. While the snake was asleep the girl carefully reached in and got the bunny out safely.

Another time she saved their field of strawberries by sprinkling a lot of white flour on the plants. Some cattle owners who lived near by insisted on herding their cattle through the strawberry field to get to a watering hole. This was back during really hard times and some people just did not care about the next guy.

The girl's father had tried to get the judge to stop the cows from crossing the strawberry field. But, the cowboys won under something called "free range".

The next time the plants got big and it was time to move the cattle the girl covered the plants with flour. When the cowboys got there they just sat on their horses and stared at the scary field.

They thought the flour was poison. They knew the cows would eat some of the plants. They turned the herd around and left and never came back. The head cowboy only uttered one word: "Pizen".

I realized I was a lot like the strawberry girl. Many of us were. Or wanted to be. The strawberry girl was definitely one of our heroes. Miz Lerner was more than a hero for reading this book, and others, to us. And for all the other things she did for us. She even went out with us at recess and would encourage us to bat the ball as hard as we could and to run the bases as fast as we could. She was our cheerleader.

Miz Lerner sure knew how to keep us happy. By reading to us. She kept us captivated and under control. She was controlling but we did not know we were being controlled. Miz Lerner was in charge.

She told us that when she was five years old she walked into her kindergarten class on the very first day and took charge of the class. She has been in charge of a class ever since.

This year, for the first time, Miz Lerner had been challenged. Or competed with. There was a set of twin girls in our class. One was quiet and reserved. The other one was extremely bossy and took charge of everything that existed. She even took charge of everything that did not exist. Leslie grabbed the world by the nose, slung it around over her head and popped it like a bull whip. Almost everything Leslie said was total fiction. She was a ram rod. Lilyan, her nice sister we called "Sweet Lily" was always truthful, dependable, a quiet delight and a good friend.

I do not know how a class could cope with Leslie without Miz Lerner there to maintain reality order and a degree of sanity. It seems Miz Lerner saw something of herself in Leslie. And it was obvious that by the time the school year was almost over Miz Lerner had developed a very deep love for Leslie.

Miz Lerner was a teacher. She was also a goddess. She ruled like a goddess. Not only in her speech and manners but also in her appearance. She wore her hair swept up smooth on the back and sides all around. There were curls and waves on the very top of her head. Each and every hair was always in the exact same spot. Not one hair moved from the day before.

She always wore crisp starched and ironed dresses. She had them done at the laundry downtown. Long sleeves in the winter. Short sleeves in the spring. She always had pockets. Big mysterious pockets that contained Lord only knows what all. She could always reach in what we called The Magic Pockets and come up with what ever was needed. A thumb tack, chalk, pencil, a clean white handkerchief, a magnifying glass, or the pitch pipe. She and those pockets were super human.

We were certain Miz Lerner never smoked, drank or cussed. Never went to the bathroom. And, was never naked.

We had no idea what her age was. We never though about it. We assumed she was the same in age and appearance from her very first day on earth and had never changed one iota. In our minds and hearts she had always looked the same. Had always been here and always would be.

THE TWINS

They looked exactly alike but that was where it ended. They were as different from each other as any two people could be. Leslie was pushy and bossy - always herding people around. On the playground she would often have kids all lined up playing some kind of game she had just invented even though they had just been playing something else. Leslie was hard to ignore. It was easier to go along with her than it was to argue with her. She had some kind of power. Maybe it was because she was so different. Most kids were fairly passive and would do mostly as they were told. Leslie reveled in this. Being in a class of thirty ten year old kids was the mother lode for such a controller as Leslie.

Her twin sister, Lilyan, was exactly the opposite. She never told anyone to do anything. She was mostly quiet but she would talk sometimes. When

Leslie would tell one of her wild tales Lilyan would not exactly back her up on it. She would just say something with real poise and grace. Like: Well, it could have happened like that.

Leslie knew how to take over our thinking. That is how she got her power. One day when it was her turn to lead the singing she told us a story about how music got started. She said in the beginning there were no notes. Then they invented the first note. It was the middle C. The first middle C was both sharp and flat. Then each year they would invent another note. It took eighty-eight years to invent music. Again, Sweet Lilyan would assure us that it could have happened like that. And we agreed that maybe it could have.

Leslie would tell us that dogs eat the bark off of trees. That is what makes them bark. Stay away from clocks that run slow or fast. Your wrist watch may catch the same disease. At night the sun turns into the moon. That is why the sun and the moon are never out at the same time.

Leslie was in charge of this universe and all other universes. The one thing she was most in charge of was her twin sister.

Lilyan had asthma. Sometimes she would stay home from school. We would ask Leslie if Lilyan would be okay. She told us her twin would get well because it was against the law for people our age to die.

No matter what Lilyan was doing Leslie insisted on showing her how to do it and doing it for her. She protected Lilyan and did everything for her. Everything.

One day Miz Lerner gave us a special assignment to do. It was a one page printed exercise. We were supposed to read the directions and do what it told us to do. Miz Lerner was not going to be explaining the directions or answering any questions. It was an exercise to see if we could read and follow directions by ourselves. We were not to talk to anyone after she told us to begin. We had fifteen minutes. As soon as Miz Lerner said, Begin, Leslie got up from her seat and went marching like the Little General all the way across the room to Lilyan's desk to her. Miz Lerner stopped the timing and said to Leslie in a firm voice to sit down at her desk and do not get up until she said so. We began again when Miz Lerner repeated, Begin.

As different as Leslie and Lilyan were from each other they were even more different from the rest of us. We had never known twins before.

Especially twins that looked exactly alike. It could have been that when Leslie looked at Lilyan she felt as though she was looking at herself in a mirror and was trying to take care of herself. We soon learned why Leslie had a great need for being in charge and doing an obnoxious amount of care taking.

Their family was from way up north. Leslie said she could run and jump across the border and be in Canada. We had never known anyone from that far North before. They were Catholic. Their parents asked that they be excused from class and go wait in the Library when the Bible study teacher came around once a week for about fifteen minutes. This was the Bible belt and their leaving class while the nice Sunday school teacher was there was downright weird to us. All she did was tell us stories and show us pictures. We did not have to believe any of it. We were very comfortable on Bible story day. We were not tested on these stories.

As different as the twins were from us their parents were even more different from the other parents in Sterling. They lived in a very nice phosphate village about five miles from town. They lived in one of the biggest and fanciest houses because the father was a really big wheel at that company. People said he was brilliant. He had gone to college and studied about mining way up North. Very few, if any of the other workers had gone to college and studied about mining. They just started out digging in the dirt and learned as they went along.

That whole family was different from us and different from each other. Both the mother and father were very attractive people. He looked like Gregory Peck in the movie Duel in the Sun. The mother looked like a movie star too. And, she knew it. She must have thought she was Irene Dunne, Greer Garson, Ida Lupino, Carole Lumbard and Myrna Loy all rolled up into one.

She never did anything other mothers did. The things she did do was stuff other mothers never did. And she looked and dressed different. She always looked like she just came from the beauty parlor. Her hair was always done up in a foreign looking way. Fresh and neat. Her clothes were obviously expensive. She was the only one who wore clothes like hers. They did not come from the stores in Sterling. Maybe Chicago or New York, we heard someone say.

When she was at home she often wore a long silky robe that was flairy. The sleeves fluttered like the wings of a giant bird. There was a row of fur down the front from neck to hem. She even had matching slippers with a ball of fur on the toes. She did not look like any mama we knew. And she did not act like any mama we knew. By the time the twins got home from school she was doing what she did most of the time. Lying on the couch smoking cigarettes and drinking alcohol. And it was obvious she had been doing this for a while. Her children did not see her very often when she was stone cold sober. It did not seem like they knew her. She rarely talked to them. The mother took up little or no time with the twins. The father took up some time with them when he was not tied up at work or out of town. He had precious little time to play with them or to just visit. But he made an effort.

About the only thing the mother said to the children was when she gave them a little shove toward the door and said, Go play. Fortunately there were a lot of kids in the village to play with. They were best friends with a thirteen year old girl down the road. She was very attentive and generous and took up a lot of time with the girls. Sometimes she would feed them at her house when the girls' parents nor the maid were at their house and no one had thought to stock the kitchen with something for them to eat.

Most people in the village knew the parents left the girls alone, with Leslie in charge, when they were in town playing cards or whatever. They called it bridge. Other parents did not leave children alone. Never.

When the parents were at home they had dinner around eight p.m. in the dining room with wine and candle light. The maid fed the children in the kitchen earlier. Around five. The children were not allowed in the dining room.

We did not know one single family that had dinner that late at night with wine and candles. Everyone in our world had dinner with the whole family around six p.m.

We saved the candles for when the electricity went off and no one could afford wine.

The mother would not have anything to do with anything that was not fancy. We called her, Miss Fancy Smancy.

Another big difference was that the twins had a younger sister about six years old. The twins were major tom boys. The younger sister was feminine and pretty. A little ballerina. The mother actually took up some time with the pretty young girl.

The twins were not pretty. They had high foreheads that collided with dark brown curly, frizzy hair that was never, ever combed. Their eyes were as dark as the inside of a cave and always seemed to be saying, I have something I need to tell you about. But I can't. I do not know how. Because I do not understand it at all.

The twins did not look anything like their little sister. They also did not look anything like their beautiful parents. We did not know who they looked like.

The mother dressed the clumsy, tomboy twins in the finest clothes. Their school clothes were entirely different from ours. New and expensive. Their clothes were like camouflage.

They looked rather strange when they went to neighborhood birthday parties dressed in satin party dresses covered in rows of satin ruffles. They were told to wear the satin dresses. They obviously dressed themselves with no supervision. To finish up their fancy ensemble they would wear big brown leather oxfords and thick white bobby socks. Somehow, satin and brown leather oxfords do not go together. We all agreed they would have looked better if they had worn their denim jeans.

We were in a phosphate village for goodness sakes.

Fancy smancy.

THE FIRE

There are twenty-four hours in a day. Why could it not have happened at any other time other than Three O'clock on a Sunday morning? Why could it not have happened at Three O'clock on a Saturday afternoon? Or during the week during the daytime when people were awake and up and around?

It was spring. The wind was blowing so hard everyone in the village were afraid the fire would spread and burn all the houses down. The people next door were watering down their house with a garden hose.

As people heard the commotion they came out of their houses to see what was going on. Most people were in shock and rather useless. The fire trucks were there. Noisy.

It was the twins' nice big house totally in flames. An old wood frame house. They call it fat pine. The twins' best friend - the teenage girl - had walked up from her house from down the road. Everyone had gotten out of the house without a scratch. Except for Lilyan. The parents had come home from their very late Saturday night as usual. They had been in town doing whatever they do in town. The twins and the younger sister had been home by themselves all afternoon and evening and late into the night. As usual.

When the parents came home the father went to bed in one of the front bedrooms. The twins were in the other front bedroom. The mother went to a newer bedroom built in the rear of the house beyond the dining area. The back bedroom had a door to the outside.

By the time the teenage girl got to the house all the members of the family were in the front yard. Except Lilyan. The mother was a mess. There had not been enough sober up time before the fire had broken out. Her fancy robe was on wrong side out. One sleeve was completely empty. Her hair wet and matted from the neighbor's hose and one of her movie star bedroom slippers was missing. One shoe on. One shoe off.

When the father realized Lilyan was still in the house he ran back in. He never came out.

Not on his own. They later carried him out in a rubber sheet.

The mother had been screaming for him to come out. There was no way he would not have tried to get his child out of the burning house. He was overcome by smoke or a beam had fallen on him.

No one knows how she got out but somehow Lilyan wound up outside. Very severely burned. Barely recognizable. Some neighbors drove her to the hospital.

The teenage girl was with Leslie and the younger sister. The father was dead. The mother was beyond consoling. Somehow Miz Lerner got word of all this and made it to the hospital before Lilyan died. She only lived for less than a day but Miz Lerner was there.

Leslie wound up at Miz Lerner's house. By Monday afternoon Miz Lerner's spare room was full of clothes and other things people had brought over for the twins and the family. The mother and young sister were staying with friends. The father and Lilyan were dead by this time. Leslie was sitting on the floor stuffing tissue paper into the toes of some nice black patent leather school shoes for Lilyan. Leslie figured they were a little bit large but would fit perfectly well with tissue paper in the toes. Leslie did not know Lilyan and her father were dead. When Miz Lerner told her she started crying. She could not stop crying. She cried for a week. Miz Lerner stayed home from her teaching job and held Leslie while she cried. This was the only time Miz Lerner had missed school. This was the only thing that could have kept her away from her classroom.

Miz Lerner was out of the classroom for a week or so. We had a substitute teacher who was very nice. When Miz Lerner came back she told us about Lilyan's injuries and about her dying in the hospital. She gave us strict orders to remember Lilyan the way she was before the fire.

In about ten days or so after the fire Miz Lerner had Leslie, the young sister and the mother come by our classroom to say good-bye. We did not know they were coming.

This whole thing already seemed like a movie script. Now it really became cosmic. The mother nor the girls said anything at all. Not even Leslie. Not one word. Miz Lerner spoke for them. They just stood there in front of the room. She said they just dropped by to say good bye before they flew way out northwest where the mother had family.

And Miz Lerner said it would be nice if we sang the song "Now is the Hour". This is the good bye song that was one of Miz Lerner's favorites. We sang it and sang it well. It was like a movie. Or an operetta. Leslie, the mother and the little sister turned and walked out of the room. Miz Lerner walked a ways down the hall with them. Gave Leslie a great big hug. It was over.

It seemed like this moment had been scripted for a long time. And it seemed like the good bye song had been written for us to learn and to sing to them at this moment. Someone or something knew this was going to happen. It was a few weeks before the end of school. We did not sing the song again.

Sometime later, Miz Lerner was over heard to say that letting Leslie go was the hardest thing she had ever had to do. Taking care of Leslie was the only thing that could have kept Miz Lerner out of her class room for a whole week. This made Miz Lerner the hero of all heroes.

BURRIS SICKLE

And then along came Burris Sickle. Who was he? Where did he come from and what in the heck was he doing in a nice town like Sterling?

He was from a big city on the west coast of the state. He was an undertaker - or funeral director - who worked at someone else's funeral home. He was also connected to an outfit that sold life insurance. These two things do not go together.

The story goes that he was married and living in the big city with his second wife. A day or two before she was fixing to go to the hospital to have their first baby something terrible happened. He "said" he was sitting at the kitchen table cleaning his shotgun when it went off accidentally. Shot her right smack kedab in the stomach. She and the baby both died instantly.

He had his wife insured for a lot of money. He came over here to the center of the state and bought some small funeral homes. Got himself another wife and was all set to start conning everyone into believing he was a very warm, kind, gentle person. It worked on almost everyone. Although some of the wisest people would say about him, There is something about him that does not meet the eye. It is a wonder more people did not say the same thing. He had most people fooled. Maybe they wanted to be fooled. He was everyone's best friend. Or they thought he was. He was too kind and too sweet to be for real.

When a woman had a baby he would drive them from the hospital to their home in his ambulance. He did not charge for this.

He would spend a tremendous amount of time with members of a family after one of them had died, especially with wealthy widows. It was obvious what he was doing but no one seemed to notice.

Everyone did notice his appearance. He was always dressed up. His shoes always looked like they were brand-new. That was unheard of in these parts. His suits were new looking too. Fresh pressed. Two toned shoes, brown and white.

It looked like he was wearing spats. Generally speaking, he was soft, mushy and prissy and he was a chain smoker. People were impressed to have a professional person for a dear friend. They overlooked the fact that he was very strange.

The first time I saw him was when I went to one of his funeral homes. A client of my father's had died. We just went by long enough to sign the book and to say good-bye. When Burris Sickle came walking across a large room to greet us he was wearing some shoes with soft soles or something. The floors were hardwood. His feet did not make a sound as he walked. Most people's shoes would have been loud. Not his. He walked and held his head and facial expression just exactly like that creepy actor, Peter Lorre. What is worse he was holding his hands in front of his stomach just like we always saw dead people in their casket. The left hand on the stomach and right hand on top of the left hand.

I was only ten years old but I knew there was something seriously wrong with him. I was not a Coyote Kid for nothing.

His first wife divorced him and ran him off. She owned some commercial property in the big city. He tried to get it put in his name when she was not looking. This did not work. So he used a more direct approach with his second wife.

Bought a lot of insurance on her then killed her with a shotgun. That worked pretty good, for a while anyway.

He had a new wife. Businesses and things were going good. He seemed to be immune to any criticism. Even when he got drunk and drove his car everywhere except on the road.

And he surely thought he had hit the jackpot when he became endeared to one of the finest families in the county. And you could not tell it by looking at them but they were also very wealthy. They were Cracker royalty. They owned several thousand acres and a large beef herd. They had a farm where they lived. The cattle ranch and ranch house were several miles away. We went there one day. We drove for miles over property owned by this great family. Everyone called them Uncle Jake and Sister Phoebe whether we were kin to them or not.

These people chose to live plain. They did not buy anything they did not have to have. Sister Phoebe made all of her clothes out of flour sacks, even her underwear. She was about four feet nine inches tall, maybe one hundred pounds. She was as tough as a rusty nail and as feisty as a mama wildcat. Uncle Jake was just as tough and as honest and dependable. Like most people around here they were direct descendants of the original pioneers who settled this area. Therefore were considered to be anointed. No one had more respect than Uncle Jake and Sister Phoebe.

Burris Sickle made a huge mistake when he thought he could do this family any harm and get away with it. He must have thought they were just some under-educated country people and he could pull anything over on them.

They were down to earth people, but they were not dumb. The only mistake they ever made was trusting someone they thought was being nice to them. Burris Sickle.

SISTER PHOEBE'S AND UNCLE JAKE'S HOME

We figured that when God created heaven and earth he also created the farmhouses like Sister Phoebe and Uncle Jake's. They looked like they had been there since day one. And there were a lot of them too. They were all exactly the same color. Which was no color at all. Never painted. All grayed boards. Everyone felt at home out in the country because all the houses were familiar.

Phoebe and Jake had a son we called Clem. He was not totally dumb, but was a little slow on the uptake. He could do work that was simple, but usually needed instructions. He would need supervision the rest of his life.

A family of colored people worked on the farm at planting and cropping time. One of their boys wound up living at the farm most of the time. He was real smart and a fine person. He had come home from the military about a year earlier. He did real good in the army. Even got a commendation saying he was a good and steady soldier.

It was his steadiness and the courage of his convictions that made him a big hero when it came time to convict Burris Sickle of Sister Phoebe's murder. The colored boy's name was John Paul.

Phoebe and Jake loved John Paul like their own boy. He had a room that was built on the end of the back porch. He ate at the dining table with them when no one else was there.

The evenings might see them all on the front porch. Resting and talking about what they did today and what they were going to do tomorrow. Sister Phoebe arocking and apoking. Jake just sitting. The boys stretched out on the floor.

This heavenly front porch was the same front porch that Sister Phoebe would meet her brutal murder at the hands of Burris Sickle.

They got mixed up with Sickle when he talked them into becoming partners in the cattle ranch. Of course he promised to always take care of their son Clem. Sickle was quite a bit younger than

Jake and Phoebe. This sounded like a good idea at the time.

They had met when Uncle Jake's brother died. Six months later Uncle Jake died. Another six months later Sister Phoebe would die too.

Before Uncle Jake died, he could tell there were a lot of calves missing from the big ranch. Sickle and Uncle Jake rode out into the pasture to check on things. Only Sickle came back alive. Later, people figured Sickle had killed Uncle Jake, too.

Our own private detective, Slip, was already looking up cases in his clippings scrapbook. He found the article about Sickle's wife and child being shot and killed. Some people already knew about his "accident". By the time Sister Phoebe was killed most everyone knew about it. Things became accelerated from here on out.

The partner agreement was that if Phoebe died, the property would go to Sickle and Clem and Sickle would be guardian of Clem. Or something like that. We all figured he would have killed Clem too if he had not gotten arrested for killing Sister Phoebe. What a mess.

THE MURDER

Uncle Jake had been dead for a few months. Sickle went by the farm regularly to see Sister Phoebe. He was married and much younger, but it looked like he was courting Phoebe. This was the way he treated all women and they would melt and run down in their shoes. He had most of the men completely bamboozled.

One evening he came over and brought some candy and some cokes. This would have been nice but there was poison in Sister Phoebe's. She started throwing up. A lot. For some reason Sickle decided he needed some gas. Why he wanted to drive miles and miles into town just to get gas was a puzzlement no one ever figured out. Sister Phoebe threw up all the way there and back. She did not get to ride in a nice big comfortable sedan very often and wanted to go riding even though she was sick.

So there they were. John Paul and Clem in the backseat. Sister Phoebe throwing up in the front seat. They had to stop the car a couple of times so Phoebe would not have to hang out the window. They got gas and headed back to the farm.

By the time they got back to the farm Phoebe was too sick for words. And of all the crazy dumb things, he told John Paul and Clem to take the farm Jeep and drive into town to the funeral home and tell the assistant on duty to bring the ambulance out to the farm. He could have taken her to the hospital in his car. He later told the Police he could not pick her up because she was too heavy. There were three men there. She was four feet nine inches and weighed less than one hundred pounds. He told John Paul and Clem not to hurry. Do not speed.

As soon as John Paul and Clem were out of sight, Sickle began beating Phoebe with a tire iron. She was sitting in her rocking chair on the front porch. She fought back. She was too much for him. She protected herself. But she was badly injured and bleeding all over the porch.

Sickle gave up on the tire iron and started choking her. He choked her until she was dead. Sister Phoebe was taken to the funeral home where

Sickle worked on her for hours trying to hide her injuries. Her clothes were completely soaked in blood. Her head and body badly bruised. He told people she had fallen and that is how she was injured.

After Phoebe was taken to the funeral home, Sickle got John Paul to get buckets of water and a broom and wash all the blood off the porch. Blood was even on the walls. He probably figured John Paul was just another dumb colored boy and would not say anything about the blood all over the porch. Probably figured he would be too scared to say anything about it. Sickle was the devil. And he was just plain stupid.

John Paul would be the only colored man to testify against a white professional man in a murder trial we ever knew about. It must have taken a tremendous amount of courage to do this. He did it because Sister Phoebe was like a Mama to him. And because he was a brave and honest man.

THE FUNERAL

I am not making this up. There was no viewing at the funeral home. There was no doctor. There was no death certificate. Sister Phoebe's family members insisted on having the lid on the casket open at the cemetery. She did not look like herself at all. Sickle had put a huge amount of wax on her face trying to cover up her wounds. She was wearing gloves. She never wore gloves. The casket was turned so her feet were to the west instead of the usual east so the lid would cast a shadow across her mutilated face. It really did not hide anything. After the service Sickle told the groundskeeper not to seal the vault. This was so she and Uncle Jake could go straight to heaven together. Uncle Jake's vault had been sealed months ago. Sickle said it had not been.

Loren was the first to notice the reversed casket. He thought it was very weird. Spooky. Melody was singing, "East is east and West is west and the wrong one he has chose". All the way home in the car. We all joined in.

Sister Phoebe's kinfolk were all raising a ruckus with the authorities. They knew she was too healthy to just up and die like that. And she did not look at all right.

Sickle told John Paul they were going to the cemetery around eleven o'clock that night to dig up Phoebe because he did not want the Police messing with her. And for him to bring two shovels.

John Paul went to the gas station where he worked sometime. The owner was someone he trusted. He told the owner Sickle had told him to dig up Sister Phoebe. The owner of the station called a deputy he knew real well.

Sickle went by the cemetery on his way to pick up John Paul. There was a deputy there who asked Sickle what was he doing there. Sickle said he was just checking on the flowers. The deputy said, "This time of night"? Sickle asked the deputy what he was doing there. He told Sickle, if they need the body for anything they wanted to make sure it was still there.

In a few days the authorities had enough evidence on Sickle to arrest him.

THE TRIAL

People came from all over. They brought food. Some used vacation time to take off from work so they could attend the trial.

The courthouse has now usurped the movie theatre. This was very exciting. It almost seemed festive. Partly because it was an undertaker on trial for murder. Partly because it was Sister Phoebe who was the one who got murdered.

The courtroom was packed. Everyone brought a buddy with them to save their seat for restroom breaks or whatever. Most people brought their lunch so they could hold their seat during lunch recess. These people were determined not to leave this room.

There were a lot of colored people outside and going up to the balcony. We had never seen colored spectators before. Very few. The only colored person connected to this trial was John

Paul. They knew John Paul was going to testify and they did not want to miss that. No siree!

One of the girls in our class was the granddaughter of the bailiff. He put a chair just inside the railing. There she was. Sitting in her ringside seat.

We had been in this courtroom a couple of times before but it sure seemed different today. Nothing seemed the same. It was more like grand central station than a courthouse.

The blind woman who ran the snack bar was wearing very red lipstick. We figured she wanted to look good even though she could not see herself. She would also rent one of those wooden crates Coca Cola bottles came in for fifteen cents a day. People who had no seat could sit on them or stand on them so they could see.

How they were able to keep order in all this mess was a miracle. But once the judge came in it became deathly quiet. Spooky.

We were able to see two or three hours of the trial after school. We ran to the courthouse. This was good timing. We got to see some of the best parts. We got to see John Paul testify about Sister Phoebe getting severely ill after eating the candy Burris Sickle gave her. And about him being ordered by Sickle to wash all her blood off the porch. And being told by Sickle to bring two shovels to the cemetery to help dig Sister Phoebe up.

This beat any movie we ever saw. John Paul was steady and brave. He was not scared at all. John Paul was proud and everyone was proud of him.

We figured there were two lawyers running this trial. The good lawyer was the prosecutor. The bad lawyer was Sickle's defense attorney. We called them Mr. Good and Mr. Mularky. Mr. Mularky was all the time telling wild tales and pulling dopey tricks. He even got down on his knees and prayed to the jury to acquit Sickle. Then he said Sister Phoebe had a seizure. Grabbed her own throat and choked herself to death.

We had to check out the balcony. We were the only white people up there. It was mostly colored women. It may have been a lot of people from John Paul's church. We could not stay up there. It was even hotter up there than downstairs. Two Pound got sick and one of the ladies was holding her in her lap and fanning her with one of those church fans. We went back downstairs.

It was me, Melody, Tough, Two Pound and Loren. Slip and Else were on their own. As usual, Loren was carrying around one of those Coke crates. He was so tiny he could not see anything without it.

By the third day of the trial we were old hands at finagling our way around. We found four seats fairly close together. I, Melody, Tough and Two Pound sat down. Loren was against the wall standing on his Coke crate. We were set.

The funeral home assistant who helped prepare Sister Phoebe was next to testify. They swore him in. He sat down. We took one look at him and the breath went out of us. And would not go back in. Oh, my Lord! It was him! Or his twin brother. His cousin. Or someone who looked just like him. It was Roy Rogers. Could it be. It might as well have been.

He testified there had been no death certificate nor a doctor for Sister Phoebe. Mr. Mularky tried every trick in the book to get this young man, Buddy Wright, to say there was a death certificate but it must have gotten misplaced. Mr. Mularky spent the next two days trying to get Buddy Wright to change his story. Buddy stood his ground. Just like our movie hero. Now we had a real live hero right here in Sterling. He also gave a detailed description of the condition of Sister Phoebe's body when she was brought to the funeral home. It was horrible to listen to.

People were asking Buddy Wright for his autograph after court was adjourned. Two Pound went up there and got him to sign a piece of notebook paper. She was pale with excitement - and the heat.

Members of the jury were totally convinced Burris Sickle murdered Sister Phoebe. They convicted him of first degree murder. He was sentenced to be executed. This execution would be carried out in a few years.

The only thing we had to deal with after the trial was Melody and Two Pound being so besotted with Buddy Wright. That is all we heard, all day, everyday. Buddy Wright. Buddy Wright. For what seemed like an eternity.

When the trial was over and we were still in the courthouse everything seemed to become super-natural. Slip and Else said they had been up in the dome of the courthouse and they saw Sister Phoebe's ghost.

After everything else that had happened this past year, it was easy to believe Sister Phoebe's ghost was indeed in the dome. We did not argue.

The next thing that happened was way beyond our comprehension. The odds of it happening was surely millions to one. Buddy Wright had gotten a job at another funeral home. It had been a few weeks after the trial. Around dusk one evening there was a knock on Melody and Two Pound's screen front porch door. Two Pound went to see who it was. She came back to Melody's bedroom where we were. Came back fast.

She said in a soft voice. It was Buddy Wright. We had a good laugh. We thought that was really funny. Yeah. Sure. Two Pound insisted. Melody looked out her window. It was Buddy Wright. No one was able to go to the door. Their father had to go see who it was.

Buddy Wright had been sent to a house in the vicinity and stopped at this well lit up house for directions. He stopped at this house while Melody and Two Pound were talking about him. Did their energy draw him to go there? What are the odds? Did his energy testifying cause Sister Phoebe to appear in the dome. What are the odds?

THE LAST PAGE

The Coyote Kids had an important meeting today. We decided we are not going to let anyone live in Sterling unless they were born and raised here. At least we are not going to allow any more weird undertakers from big cities to come live here.

We figured things like the fire and Sister Phoebe would not happen again. Things that bad only happen once.

We investigated the fire for a long time. Some people said the fire probably started in the ceiling exhaust fan in the living room. We decided the fire started at the gas tank that was just below the window next to Lilyan's bed. A plume of gas leaked out. The wind was blowing so hard it caused a static spark. The gas exploded. The ceiling fan pulled the fire through the window onto Lilyan. That is why she was burned so severely right away and why no one else was burned initially. All of

Lilyan's burns were on her head, face, chest and forearms. None on her back or legs. We think she was lying on her left side. Facing the window. There was a gas stove on the other side of the wall the head of her bed was up against. She was surrounded by gas.

Then we went out under the trees behind Melody's house. Built a campfire and cooked our supper. We had hot dogs, beans and bacon and cocoa.

We spread our bedrolls around the fire. Melody and Tough brought their horses over and tied them to the trees. The horses slept a little and just hung around while we slept longer. The horses knew they were pacifying us. We used saddles for pillows. Just like in the movies.

We were all together tonight. Even Else. Although he may disappear at any moment. Slip was completely covered up. We assumed that was him under his blanket. Two Pound's sleeping bed was twice as big as she was. Loren had a very precise, efficient fire ablazing.

Sometimes when we were all together time would stop. Just for us. So as we lay there we knew for sure we would always be together. We would always live in Sterling. The movie theatre and Roy Rogers and Trigger would always be there for us. The town would always be there with all its people. The horses would always be there and everywhere. Miz Lerner would always be our teacher.

And best of all: we would always be ten years old.

ABOUT THE AUTHOR

Charlotte Crawford is a native of Polk County, Florida and is an eleventh generation Cracker.

Grew up in a small town where people did not lock their doors and the high school produced many state-wide and national notables, over-achieving doctors and incredibly talented musicians. Her life around phosphate villages is invaluable to her ability to write about Cracker lore.

She has led the typical quirky and varied life of a future writer...engineering drawing, accountant, real estate broker and a long stint in community theatre. Has written and performed songs and comedy. Considers herself to be a story teller and author. A graduate of Florida Atlantic University. Changed her major so many times she has a minor's worth is just about everything.

CPSIA information can be obtained at www.ICGtesting.com
Printed in the USA
LVOW031236210911

247244LV00004B/1/P